Targeting Music

Year 3

Dorothy Taylor
and
William McVicker

Illustrated by John Minnion

SCHOTT
EDUCATIONAL
PUBLICATIONS

British Library Cataloguing-in-Publication Data.
A catalogue record of this book is available from the British Library

ED 12458
ISBN 0 946 535 98 1

Designed and typeset by Geoffrey & Marion Wadsley
Music set by Jack Thompson
Cover design by John Minnion

The publishers would like to expresss their gratitude to the National Gallery for
permission to reproduce the picture of Doge Leonardo Loredon by Bellini (p. 60)

The authors and publisher would like to thank Peter Nickol for his invaluable
assistance in preparing this project for publication

Contents

Introduction

Although The National Curriculum is a guiding light in the preparation of this series, *Targeting Music* also looks to the Scottish Office Education Department's National Guidelines for the Expressive Arts, as well as to those for the National Curriculum for Wales, and at good education practice in general.

The *Targeting Music* series has been conceived from the outset as a comprehensive, year-by-year course which takes children on a musical journey from Reception Year onwards through the essential ways of experiencing music: listening, composing and performing. The same format has been adopted for *Targeting Music* Years 3 and 4, covering the lower junior stage. In Year 4 continuity is preserved, whilst the increasing demands and expectations provide progression.

You will wish to follow your own and your school's practice in recording achievement-levels. However, each lesson in this book ends with some suggested points of observation, and these can serve as a basis (or point of departure) for general or individual record-keeping.

There is a planned progression through the series; there is also a planned progression both through the modules and through each book. The six modules and the six lessons which comprise each book are designed to allow the teacher to follow the course throughout the school year. Thus the first term begins by focusing on children's voices and good singing principles (Module 1) moving through a similar approach to instrumental music-making (Module 2). This enables children to develop their technical skills in order to facilitate music-making both using their voices and on a range of tuned and untuned percussion instruments.

For the second term, Module 3 deals with an approach to improvising and composing, exploring voices, instruments and sounds and the communication of these ideas to others through rehearsal to performance. Module 4 deals with musical symbols and notations and a further word about this particular module is necessary.

The subject of notation is a complex one to introduce, and some of the intricacies of the relative concepts of pitch and duration have necessarily been simplified for the present. Module 4, therefore, engages in a structured approach to learning both to read and write music, through graphic representation before moving to conventional notation.

In the third term, Module 5 concerns the understanding, knowledge and appraising of music, using familiar as well as less familiar material. Particular emphasis is given to placing music into an historical context. Module 6 is designed for the end of the school year with the focus on a musical production.

Educators have rightly questioned dependency upon conventional Western musical notation. Being a musician is not solely reliant upon being able to read music. Some musicians, particularly in the fields of folk, jazz, popular music and world music do not require conventional notation, but the treasures of Western art-music do need a fuller understanding of it. The authors, therefore, have chosen to introduce conventional notation in this book. This approach has also been designed to enable teachers to approach the subject of notation with a degree of confidence.

The ability to read musical notation enables us to unlock and perform the treasures of our international musical heritage. Furthermore, it empowers teachers and pupils to approach the subject of music with greater confidence. It is also a skill which is complementary to popular music forms (and other styles) and strengthens our understanding and ability to perform, compose, enjoy and interpret music of *all* types.

It is important to remember to treat the voice in the same way that one treats an instrument – with care and attention. The voice, like an instrument, responds to being warmed up before it will work well and perform in tune. All too often in choirs and classrooms, scant attention is paid to the need to prepare the voice to sing. Difficulties encountered when encouraging children to sing often lead to frustration on the part of the teacher, when, in fact, the remedy is a simple one. Preparation in the form of warming up can help the voice, and a short time using some of the exercises in Module 1 should be beneficial to many of the lessons which follow.

The five lessons and review session which comprise Module 2 are essentially about developing pupils' confidence and fluency in instrumental performing, using tuned percussion in particular. Such aims can best be realized when schools have an adequate stock of tuned percussion instruments which are in good condition. This stock should provide at least one instrument between two children and should ideally include soprano, alto and bass glockenspiels, metallophones and xylophones together with a set of chime bars. Simple bass bars are a useful addition to this stock.

Felt-headed beaters are normally used for xylophones, wooden or plastic ones for glockenspiels and rubber or fibreglass for chime bars. In the case of bass metallophones and xylophones, beater heads are normally wrapped in wool. Developing posture and balance when playing percussion instruments enables each child to develop the use of both hands. Time spent developing this encourages lightness and dexterity.

Time is also required to practise and explore such instruments, building up technique gradually. This requires time within sessions and the use of an area where instruments are available for individual and group use. Excellent, detailed advice on tuned percussion instruments and instrumental technique is provided in *Strike Five: An Introduction to Early Classroom Work with Tuned Percussion Instruments* by Peter Sidaway in Schott's 'Beaters' series (ED12164).

There are three particular features explored in this book: the development of the principles of good singing, a structured approach to dramatic expression, culminating in the show *Cinderella*, and the introduction of conventional notation.

With respect to dramatic expression and music theatre, two main activities are presented here. Firstly, the reconstruction of a Venetian Coronation around 1600. This will help children to recognize how such historical music reflects the time and place in which it is created. The second activity is the reinterpretation of *The Sorcerer's Apprentice.*

In Margaret Rolf's operetta *Cinderella,* the children have the opportunity to engage in dialogue, songs and acting which culminate in a full performance of the piece. This activity puts into practice the skills acquired throughout the preceding modules: the voice and preparation of it, performance and instrumental technique, emphasizing and practising the skills required for presentation and performance.

There are also other related activities: drama in the Black Cat round, acting and singing ostinati in Module 1, the completion of the scene for The *Sorcerer's Apprentice* in Module 5, and exploration of atmospheric effects in Module 3 Lesson 2.

Throughout the book the text often invites teachers to work towards a performance in front of others. This is most likely to be a group performing to other members of the class. It is important for children to understand that the experience of performance also includes preparation, rehearsing, refining, and striving for quality when presenting the material to an audience.

The authors suggest that teachers use another larger space to try out a song or an activity, so that the groups can face one another to hear clearly what they are doing. In addition, teachers might more often perform the results of a lesson at an assembly, as a centrepiece or perhaps as a preface to such a gathering. The act of performing should become an intrinsic part of the musical air that children breathe.

Dorothy Taylor and William McVicker

Musical learning

Singing technique: posture, breathing, 'warming up' the voice

Pitch awareness when singing

Legato singing; phrasing

Terminology: phrase, legato

Performing a song; shaping a phrase; pitching an octave leap

Part-singing; a round

Get ready to sing

The activities below can be repeated in a shorter form at the start of any lesson in which singing will form a part.

Posture

Ask the children to imagine they are sitting on a narrow brick wall.

They should sit up straight without stiffness and without looking like a soldier, so that air from the lungs has a clear passage.

Keep the head and shoulders relaxed – drop the shoulders.
Encourage your group to prepare themselves for singing.

Breathing

Encourage slow, deep breathing before they sing – the breath should be a fat abdominal breath, rather than a short, panting breath in the upper part of the chest. Encourage quiet, natural breathing; this in turn encourages the shoulders to stay relaxed.

Ask your pupils to take a relaxed inward breath and then to hum a low note while you count to four.

This can be repeated to 'nn', or 'oo'. Go upwards by semitones as far as G. This will warm up the lower register of the voice.

For the next exercise, encourage a relaxed approach which avoids tension. Here, too, the aim is to warm up the voice.

Trad. arr. WRM

Ask your children to sing smoothly to introduce the concept of *legato* (smooth) singing. It is the joining together of notes in this fashion which gives rise to a musical phrase. For added interest, here is a possible piano accompaniment (see Appendix, p. 94 for transpositions):

Trad. arr. WRM

Invent your own exercises which suit the skills of your class, and which suit your personal interaction with your singers. Lead the singing yourself, or accompany the class using piano or guitar. If you have a good singer in your class ask him or her to help you to teach the music to the others.

Focus your attention on breathing and *legato* singing. Use descending scales rather than ascending ones to warm up, as this allows the voice to remain relatively relaxed.

Start the exercise above either at the pitch as written or on the B flat above middle C, and ascend through semitones to D major or E flat major.

A good, fun exercise for the mouth and lips is this one:

Use some of these exercises before singing songs. Vary your routine.

White swans

This song has a number of benefits, and presents the opportunity to apply points already discussed:

- It encourages smooth (*legato*) singing.
- It needs to be sung in one breath. Sing it at a reasonable pace, and make sure your singers' shoulders stay relaxed. Point out to your class that this long line of music is known as a *phrase*.
- It introduces a difficult octave leap at the start of bar 2. Encourage the children to sing intervals accurately by listening carefully to themselves.

Trad. arr. WRM

White swans go   sail-ing a-long,   sail-ing a-long,   sail-ing a-long.

Start by learning *White swans* as a class. Try breaking the phrase down into smaller units in order to learn it, but always be clear about what constitutes a *phrase*.

Sing it to them, ensuring that you do so as accurately as possible yourself. An accurate role model encourages pupils to sing well. If the leader (the teacher or some children) sings with the right inflection – legato, in one breath, and perhaps with a little crescendo into the octave leap to give a sense of musical direction – the class will have a good model to follow.

Performing

When the group has mastered the exercise – and only then – divide them into two groups to introduce the idea of singing a round. It will be easier for the class to sing in two parts once they are confident about the single line.

Then, if your class has done well with the two-part round, try asking them to sing it in four parts as shown on p. 8. (The numbers in the music indicate the points of entry for each part.)

Remember to keep repeating the music when the singers reach the end of the phrase, maintaining the momentum and rhythm of the line. For contrast begin again softly.

Encourage the class to stand and sing to each other in order to hear their sound clearly. Singers in a large group often do not hear the sound that they are producing, and intonation and ensemble are compromised. Ask the class to stand facing each other or in a circle. The act of moving from a 'learning' position to a 'performing' position will add excitement to what the group is doing.

Assessment points

Assess the ability of the class in *White swans* to:
◆ take a natural, relaxed breath to start to sing. (Avoid shouting 'Breathe!')
◆ sing the whole exercise in one phrase and one breath.
◆ pitch accurately, particularly the octave leap at bars 1–2.
◆ make a crescendo through the first bar to help to reach the high note.
◆ enunciate the words.

Musical learning

Awareness of rhythm and metre; rhythmic singing

Structure: call and response

Improvising: adding melody to a rhythmic phrase

Dynamics: awareness and control of loud and quiet

Using the same call-and-response structure to perform (wordless) rhythms

Exploring different percussive effects and body sounds

The name game

Listening and responding

Sit with your class in a circle. Recall some of the warm-up exercises and objectives in Lesson 1. Ask a child to sing his or her name on one note and ask the class to sing it back, exactly as they heard it. Go round the class, encouraging the singing on one note and the repetition of the note, together with the rhythm patterns that each pupil used.

Encourage the group to follow the soloist's rhythm when they respond. For example, 'My name is Tom' has two beats' rest between the soloist and the response. This seems to be a natural time-lapse between the solo line and the response. Not all names work so neatly, of course, but try to encourage this rhythmic response as it will help the game to flow along.

Most names will fit into the general 3/4 structure of the game. Follow the chorus's response with the next soloist, such that the 3/4 time is preserved. Some examples are shown below.

This game can be extended by adding the child's age (after his or her name) for the class to repeat.

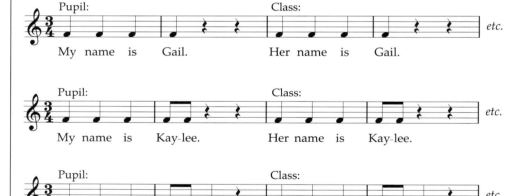

Improvising

When all the children have had several opportunities to sing, introduce the following variation. Ask the children to improvise a tune on their name.

The corporate activity of repeating pitches and rhythm focuses the ear on what is happening. Encourage inventiveness in the improvised melody. Children might, for example, sing the class names back loudly or quietly as well as using more complex melodies, whilst always using one breath to do so.

Recall good posture and breathing from Lesson 1. Also point out to the class that they are developing their own musical phrase.

Rhythmic extension

Explore the same process with rhythms only. A soloist can tap out or clap a rhythm and the class responds, maintaining the rhythmic impetus as described earlier.

Vary the dynamics and the speed. You can introduce these concepts (when it is your turn to perform in the game) without taking time to explain them, picking ideas up at the end of the class in a recapitulation of what was done. Actions introduced in this way in music often do not need further explanation.

Another variation might be to use parts of your body or the floor to achieve a variety of percussive effects and sounds: use your hands, head, thighs, cheeks, or tap the floor with your palms or knuckles.

Try to keep the speed of the game up. If it gets faster ask the children if they noticed this tendency themselves. What was it that encouraged this to happen? You might consider introducing finger clicks to keep the rhythms stable.

Assessment points

◆ Were the children able to maintain the rhythmic impulse? If not, explore which names upset the rhythmic flow and why this was so.
◆ Did the children exhibit a tendency to get faster?
◆ How did the group respond to improvisation? Were they able to repeat complex improvisations? If so, try to focus in on what encouraged it. If not, why was this so? Was it because the rhythmic impetus was upset or the improvisation deviated from a strong rhythmic flow?

Black cat

Musical learning

Learning and performing a song

Controlling phrasing, dynamics and articulation when singing

Terminology: piano, forte, legato, staccato

Structure: use of contrasting phrase-lengths and articulations

Musical dialogue and drama

Pitch control: a rising 4th

Extension: more complex part-singing; improvising actions to underline musical drama

Performing

Warm up with some exercises from Lesson 1. Begin by humming and then vocalize, especially if this lesson is used early in your teaching day. Remind your singers of the benefits of good posture, and recall the principles outlined in Lesson 1.

Learn this song as a class. As with *White swans* in Lesson 1, ensure that the group has grasped the principles of phrasing. Teach the song first in the same way as in Lesson 1: either phrase by phrase (sung by the teacher as the class responds), or with a soloist or a group of singers to help the teaching process.

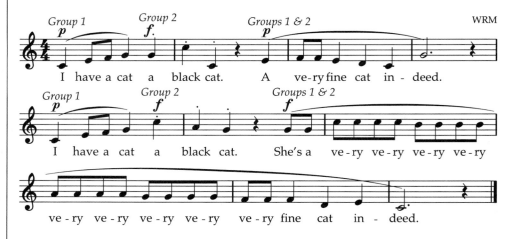

2. I know a goose, a bad goose,
   a very bad goose indeed . . .
3. I know a hen, an old hen,
   a very old hen indeed . . .
4. I know a dog, a fast dog,
   he's very very fast indeed . . .

Once the song has been learned, split your singers into two groups. One group sings the first phrase and the second group replies. Objectives here are:
- to differentiate between phrases of different length;
- to contrast the dynamics (*piano* and *forte*);
- to use different articulations (*legato* and *staccato*).

When singing this song, the class will begin to engage in a musical dialogue. The concept of repetition (explored in the Name Game in Lesson 2), now gives way to something of a musical drama. This theme will be explored further in subsequent modules throughout the book.

Ask the two groups to enact the song to each other from opposite sides of the room. When they have done this, change the groups over so that everyone experiences the different articulations, dynamics and phrase lengths.

Group 1 sing quietly (*piano*) and smoothly (*legato*).
Group 2 reply with short durations (*staccato*) and loudly (*forte*).

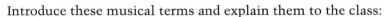

Ask the class to describe the effects that can be found in the song:
- quiet singing
- loud singing
- smooth singing
- short notes

Introduce these musical terms and explain them to the class:
- *piano*
- *legato*
- *forte*
- *staccato*

Encourage your pupils to use these technical musical terms, a musical vocabulary, rather than simply to describe what they hear.

Extension

This song works as a 2-part, 3-part and 4-part round. This is shown in the Appendix (p. 95). Adapt this song to your class's ability.

Encourage your class to invent or improvise their own actions and make this a performance activity. Take care that the dramatic element does not distract from the musical objectives.

Develop an awareness in your class that as performers they should keep in time with the other groups. You should conduct the music, and keep the ensemble together. Consider allowing members of the class to have a go at leading (or conducting) the performance.

Consider asking the class to make a recording of their performance, either on tape or even on video. What could they improve? What did they like?

Assessment points

- Were the children able to effect a marked contrast in phrases, articulations and dynamics?
- What were they best at?
- What were they less good at?
- Can they remember the definitions of *forte*, *piano*, *staccato*, *legato*?
- Can they use these terms confidently?
- How well did they perform the awkward intervals (bars 1–2)?

Shalom Chaverim

Musical learning

Learning and performing a song; shaping the performance through awareness and control of breathing, dynamics, pitch, phrasing

Terminology and notation: crescendo, diminuendo

Part-singing: 3-part round; encouraging awareness of what other parts are doing

Performing to others; inventing actions to go with a performance

Use some of the warm-up exercises from Lesson 1 and ask your class to sing the *White swans* round from the same lesson, using this as a way of warming up the singers' voices. Remind your class of the need to take care when pitching the difficult octave interval.

The Israeli round *Shalom Chaverim* that follows, has some challenging features:
- it covers a wider vocal range;
- it has sustained top notes;
- it needs to be sung *legato* and *sostenuto* (sustained);
- the dynamics need to be controlled.

When the children are ready, teach the song line by line, or perhaps using some of your good singers to help you. As with the Name Game in Lesson 2, maintain a sense of rhythm as you teach the class a line; in other words, ask them to repeat what you sing, and wherever possible avoid interrupting their response.

Training a class to respond in this rhythmic way is a useful tool both for teaching and thinking about music. Ensure, too, that *Shalom Chaverim* is taught to the class as musically as possible:
- introduce a gradual *crescendo* up to bar 3;
- make a *diminuendo* from half way through bar 5 to the end;
- follow the breathing suggestions in the music to control the phrases and remind the group about good phrasing.

Use the board in the classroom to illustrate the way musicians write a *crescendo* and a *diminuendo*. Ask your pupils to have a go at drawing their own dynamic markings on paper, perhaps over the words of the song. Define these words for them:

crescendo	getting louder	![crescendo hairpin]
diminuendo	getting softer	![diminuendo hairpin]

crescendo

Fare|well my friends, fare|well my friends, fare|well, fare|well!

diminuendo

Un|til we meet a|gain my friends, fare|well, fare|well!

Sha - lom Cha-ve-rim! Sha - lom Cha-ve-rim! Sha - lom, Sha - lom! Le -
Fare - well my__ friends, fare - well my__ friends, fare - well, fare - well! Un -

- hit - ra - ot, le - hit - ra - ot, Sha - lom, Sha - lom!
- til we__ meet a - gain my__ friends, fare - well, fare - well!

Only when the song is learned, with dynamics and phrasing, should the class be split into two groups to begin to sing the round. Each group will need to take extra care when pitching the interval of a fourth which leads to the top notes.

Adding dynamics and phrasing *after* a piece has been learned will never be quite as successful as applying all the musical features at the point of learning. Try to make the musical inflections an intrinsic element of the music.

When the class has mastered the round in two parts, try splitting them into three groups. Ask them to stand in three groups so that they can hear clearly what the other groups are singing. Maintaining the musical ensemble will be difficult for the children unless they can develop an awareness of what the other groups are doing.

Performing to others

In order to help your class to understand what it is to perform the music, ask them to move to different parts of the room, or, as suggested in an earlier lesson, move to another room, perhaps the school hall with its different acoustic. Ask them to face one another as they sing, so that each group can hear what the other is doing.

The performance of this piece in three parts, with the groups standing in three places, suggests a musical drama. Ask each group to invent their own actions and to perform to each other as well as to an audience.

Assessment points

◆ Were the children able to maintain the rhythm of the piece as it was taught to them phrase by phrase?
◆ Were they able to make the *crescendo* and *diminuendo*?
◆ Can they remember what signs are used to represent them?
◆ Do they understand the concept of a phrase which is to be sung in one breath?
◆ Were they able to divide into three groups and maintain the ensemble?
◆ Did they deal effectively with the difficulties the song presents?

Introducing ostinato

Musical learning

Structure: ostinati

Performing six vocal ostinati, in sequence, in combinations, and accompanied by a bass line

Pitch control: octave leaps

Controlling varied dynamics

Inventing actions to accompany the music

Performing to others; assessment and refinement of a performance

Extension: more complex part-singing

In the previous lessons in this module, three rounds have been introduced: *White swans, Black cat, Shalom Chaverim*. In a round, the music can be sung almost indefinitely, until the leader chooses to finish the performance.

An ostinato has some affinity with a round, in that it is a short 'cell' of music which is featured many times. A definition of an ostinato might be 'a rhythmic or melodic figure which is persistently repeated'.

An ostinato is usually introduced as an instrumental activity, but here a purely vocal ostinato is offered. The ostinato in this lesson has been designed to be used in various ways.

In Lesson 4, a round in three parts was introduced. Here, there are six sections; it is not essential to use all six ostinato cells, and you can choose those that suit your class size and ability. Ostinatos B and C, for example, are easier than the others. By selecting some or all of these phrases a degree of differentiation can be introduced.

Use the warm-ups from Lesson 1 and then move to 'cell' A of the example given below. The class should be taught the cell and encouraged to repeat it several times. Divide your class into two and ask each group to sing it in turn, without disrupting the rhythmic flow.

The six ostinatos are presented below as A, B, C, D, E and F.

The phrases can be sung all at the same time, or they can be run together to form a song, A + B + C + D + E + F. Adapt the music to suit your class.

Encourage a musical approach to the phrases:
- sing in one breath;
- encourage accuracy in the octave leap in A and E;
- sing with different dynamics: first time *forte* (loud), second time *piano* (soft);
- encourage accuracy in singing the rhythms;
- ask the groups of singers to listen to what the other groups are doing so that the resultant ensemble is good (this can be done by sitting the groups together in one large circle).

Ask the children to be inventive about making up their own actions to suit the phrases. Here are some suggestions as a starting point:

Cell	Bar 1	Bar 2
A	point finger to another group	shrug shoulders
B	point to singer's body	make imaginary horns with fingers
C	use feet as hooves	put hands on hips
D	make falling imaginary rain	repeat action
E	point up and down with notes	repeat action
F	stamp feet on each note	repeat action

There is a walking bass accompaniment to this song, shown below. If any members of your class are learning the piano, they may take it in turns to play this walking bass. Alternatively, it might be played on another suitable instrument, such as the bass xylophone.

Walking bass:

Performing to others

As with the other lessons, work towards a performance, either in the classroom or perhaps in a larger room. Encourage your groups to evaluate each other's performances. Ask the class if they can suggest ways in which they could improve their performance. If time allows, record the performance and ask the children what they like and dislike about it. Can it be improved by attention to:
- dynamics?
- phrasing?
- care when pitching?
- any other considerations?

Extension

These *ostinatos* can also be sung as a round. You can use two or three groups for this. The children will have to learn the music as a song (A + B + C + D + E + F), rather than one cell per group. The entries of the round come every two bars. Using the music in this way is more difficult than piecing together the ostinati.

Assessment points

♦ Were the singers able to maintain the ensemble? Were they listening to each other?
♦ Did the children sing the larger intervals accurately?
♦ Were they able to sing *forte* and then *piano*?
♦ Were the groups able to maintain their own cell?

Musical learning

Listening: Britten, Bizet

Structure: awareness of structure in the Britten piece – canon (round), sectional structure – diagrammatic representation of structure

Instruments: identifying the sound of a harp

Encouraging use of musical terms when describing the music

Listening

In the last five lessons the matters listed below have been dealt with.

Performing:
- preparing the voice to sing by warming up;
- understanding what a musical phrase is, and developing the skill to sing it in one breath;
- maintaining rhythmic momentum when learning music;
- using answering phrases (*Black cat*), and developing of timing and response in performance.

Listening:
- learning to sing more complex intervals by listening and repeating;
- listening to each other or another group when singing;
- introducing musical features at the learning point rather than adding them on afterwards.

Dynamics and articulations:
- *crescendo* and *diminuendo*
- *legato* and *staccato*

Improvising:
- Improvising rhythms and melody in the Name Game

Musical form and structure:
- rounds
- ostinati

This lesson draws together some of these features through listening extracts.
Ask the children to listen to 'This Little Babe' from Benjamin Britten's *A Ceremony of Carols*. This is a fast and energetic piece in which the composer treats the melody as a two-part canon (or round) following a harp interlude; after a second harp interlude it appears as a three-part round. The effect is a busy and exciting set of echo effects within the music.
- Can the class describe what they hear?
- Can the class hear how many groups of singers there are? (two or three singing as a round – sometimes known as a canon)
- Can the class hear that this is a round (or canon)?
- What instrument provides the accompaniment? (a harp)

Ask the children to see if they can identify what is happening. If they find difficulty with the speed of the music, ask them to listen for the top notes that the choir sings at the highest point of each phrase. When sung as a round these appear at different times and may prove to be a more obvious focal point for the ear.

In the first section there are three main phrases where the singers take a breath. Can the class identify how many phrases there are?

* This symbol refers to the supplementary CD, showing the appropriate track number.

Ask the children to help you draw the structure of this music on the board. You should work towards a diagram which might look something like the one below.

CHOIR

HARP

(Intro) Verse 1 (Interlude) Verse 2 (Interlude) Verse 3

2 Remind your class of 'Carillon' from Bizet's *L'Arlésienne* (used in *Targeting Music* Year 1.)

Assessment points

◆ Could the class hear how many groups of singers were involved in the Britten?
◆ Did they identify that this is a round?
◆ Did they use technical terms to describe what was happening in the music?

Om pom poddledum

Performing

Sing and play the following song to the class, using an alto xylophone.

Repeat it, encouraging the children to join in the singing. Invite a child to play a vibraslap, cymbal or gong as a feature at the end.

Tell the children that, working with a partner, they are now going to provide an accompaniment. Distribute an alto or bass instrument, or set of C, G and A chime bars, to each pair. A piano could also be added to the ensemble.

Practise first without beaters. Demonstrate this by tapping a steady beat whilst singing the song. Then, taking turns, ask one of the pair to find C. Count in over four beats, before the ensemble performance of a steadily repeated C (or *doh*) on every beat.

Encourage them to count ♩ ♩ ♩ ♩ | ♩ ♩ ♩ ♩ |
                          1 2 3 4   1 2 3 4

as they play, until it is internalized.

Try using the last bar of the melody as an introduction. Count four beats in.

Next, double the speed of the repeated C, from crotchets to quavers. Count '1 and 2 and 3 and 4 and'.

Repeat until it can be done without counting aloud. Ration the practice time by alternating turns.

Challenge half the class to respond to the other half's performance, or group to group.

Musical learning

Learning and singing a song; performing it with two different ostinato accompaniments

Tuned percussion playing technique, using two beaters

Extension: playing a tune by ear, using tuned percussion; playing it from notation; assessing an appropriate tempo for an accompaniment

Composing a melodic ostinato

Listening: Prokofiev

Next, explain that the class is going to explore another simple ostinato figure (following up module 1 lesson 5). This is on two notes, G and A, using running eighth notes or quavers. This requires two beaters to ensure smooth movement from A to G. Encourage slow practice, asking the children to bounce the beaters lightly on the middle of the bar, with a flexible wrist. (See p. 31.) Practise slowly at first and then gradually more quickly.

Extension

Invite the children, when taking turns on the instruments, to try to play the melody by ear. Provide the notated melody with the letter names below. Ask them to play the two-note G A accompaniment and to try to play it at different speeds (tempos), making judgements about which they believe to sound most appropriate.

Composing in groups

Ideally in groups of four, ask the children to compose a melodic ostinato which sounds as full of movement as the one with which they have been experimenting. Give them a range of notes covering the pentatonic scale G A B D E. Some children may wish to use recorders.

 At an appropriate point play the 'Troika' from *Lieutenant Kijé* by Prokofiev to show how this composer achieves a strong sense of movement.

Critical appraisal

Ask the groups to present their work to the rest of the class for discussion. Ask the class questions such as:
- What do you like about each ostinato pattern?
- How many people are playing the ostinato? Do they play together, separately, in turn?
- Which notes have they used for their ostinato?
- Can you play any of the ostinatos that you have heard?

Assessment points

- ◆ Are the children able to co-ordinate their hands with reasonable dexterity?
- ◆ How enthusiastically and readily do children explore, adapt and make judgements?
- ◆ How many children are able to reproduce other children's ostinatos?
- ◆ Were the children able to accompany the melody with a sense of ensemble playing?

    Use the critical appraisal period as the basis for assessing and recording group progress and achievement in relation to the task set.

My paddle's clean and bright

Performing

After vocal warm-up, teach the children to sing the traditional round *My paddle's clean and bright*.

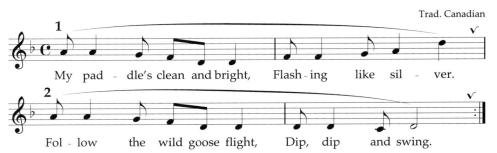

An interesting accompaniment pattern is to be found in the last bar of the round. Teach the children first to sing and then to play this as a melodic ostinato all the way through. Divide the class into three and take turns to play the accompaniment. Use it as an introduction, played twice.

Build up other ostinati accompaniments, such as this two-part drone, either played by one individual or by two on tuned percussion:

Position the players in such a way that they can see each other's arm movements. Pair the children to enable them to help each other.

Composing extension

Enable small groups to explore the many ostinato accompaniments that they can devise using the notes of the tonic chord D F A – e.g. bubbly, watery patterns such as:

Building on this work – and the language evoked such as 'shimmering, rippling, flowing' – develop composition on the water theme. Suggest that groups use a combination of tuned and untuned instruments to create an 'Underwater Piece' which could (but does not have to) include words.

Musical learning

Learning and performing a round; part-singing; performing it with two different ostinato accompaniments

Rhythmic awareness – fitting together contrasting rhythm patterns

Structure: deriving an accompaniment pattern from the song's melody

Composing extension: devising more ostinati from a given chord; developing a composition on an expressive theme, using tuned and untuned instruments and voices

Listening: Saint-Saëns (Carnival of the Animals); relating this to their composing

Notation of pupils' compositions

Include the voice as another instrumental colour, and use the potential of other available instruments to enable children to produce imaginative work. At an early point in this activity ask the class to listen to 'Aquarium' by Saint-Saëns (from *Carnival of the Animals*) to discern how he produces a similar effect.

Encourage the children to notate their compositions in whichever form they agree before presenting and tape recording them.

Assessment points

◆ How well do children co-ordinate their instrumental ostinato part with the singing group?

◆ How imaginative are the ideas for ostinatos?

◆ How well do individuals and groups present their results to others?

Musical learning

Learning and performing a song; clear articulation of words

Metre: understanding and performing a change of metre, from 4/4 to 3/4 and back; internalizing metre

Melodic shapes and structure – recognizing and identifying melodic cells

Playing a tune by ear on tuned percussion; tuned percussion technique using two beaters

Structure: ABA (ternary) form

Performing to an audience; adding untuned percussion, and dance movements

Extension: another song; more playing by ear

Song of the Eskimos

Performing

After warming up the children's voices, teach them to sing the *Song of the Eskimos* reminding them of articulation, phrasing and the good principles of singing advocated in Module 1.

Encourage them to experience the contrasting aspects of this ABA or *ternary form* by providing a rhythmic accompaniment as follows:

Section A	PAT	CLAP	CLAP	CLAP
	1	2	3	4
Section B	PAT	CLAP	CLAP	
	1	2	3	

In each case, mark the first beat strongly.

Listening and appraising

When known, discuss the shape of the melody.
- How could we show its contour with our hands?
- Where do sounds repeat?
- Where do they move and in which direction?
- Which are the important notes and why? (There is a strong feeling of BAG – or *me, ray, doh* – and this figure becomes emphasized through repetition.)
- How many times does the B A G figure occur?

Practising

Working in pairs, encourage children to work out how to play the tune with two beaters, guiding them to the most comfortable distribution between left hand and right hand. Advise them to isolate each bar of the music, slowly playing while singing to letter names (or *sol-fa-*syllables if you use them). Bringing the children together to rehearse as a class, continue section by section, not forgetting that section A repeats the first time round. Identify with the class its structure, i.e. ABA (ternary) form.

Performing to an audience

Add untuned percussion instruments such as guiro, Indian bells or triangles on the first beat of each bar. Divide the class into two halves – a singing group and an accompanying instrumental group.

Ask the singers to perform their pat, clap, clap, clap, action during the first 4/4 section, and to join hands in a circle and dance in and out to the music of the 3/4 section as they sing. Alternate parts. Rehearse, and later perform to another class, in assembly time or at a special event.

Extension

Here is another simple traditional song for children to learn vocally before attempting to play by ear. Again guide the children in working out how to distribute the tune efficiently between both hands.

Russian dance

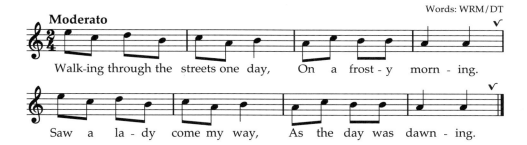

Assessment points

◆ How able are individuals at analysing the melodic construction of *Song of the Eskimos?*
◆ How quickly do the children learn to play the pieces?
◆ How do individual children contribute to shaping and polishing a piece for presentation to others?

Two very different melodies

Musical learning

Metre: awareness of contrast between swaying 3-time and march-like 4-time rhythms

Melody: moving by step and by leap

Musical character: contrast between two melodies with very different characters

Performing: tuned percussion playing technique; playing a drone accompaniment

Singing: controlling wide leaps at the start of Hot cross buns

Structure of Hot cross buns, *a melody built from highly contrasting phrases*

Performing with musical variety, e.g. dynamics; underlining the structure with contrasting instrumentation

Performing

First do some class vocal warm-up exercises as suggested in Module 1 lesson 1.

Ask the children to sway and gently tap the rhythm of this old Spanish tune as you sing it to 'la', accompanied by a light D and A drone on a bass xylophone. Then teach it phrase by phrase, asking the children to sing to 'la'.

Old Spanish tune

Drone accompaniment:

Listening and appraising

Focus on the way in which the melody moves. Invite the class to trace its contour in the air. Ask them:
- Does the melody move mostly by step or mostly by leap? (mostly by step)
- In how many places does it move in small leaps? (four)
- Put up your hands when it moves by leap.
- How many notes are used in this melody? (five, D E F G A, a pentatonic scale)

Performing

Teach the children, as in the previous lessons, to play this tune, phrase by phrase, noting where it is more comfortable to play adjacent notes with the same beater. Ask a group to play the drone accompaniment.

26

Next we have a very different tune – one that the children may well know.

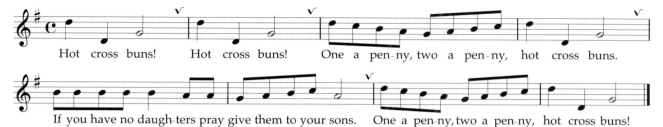

Pay particular care, when singing, to the tuning of the first three notes. Again, encourage the children to trace the contour of the melody in the air.

Listening and appraising

Afterwards pose questions as before:
- Does the first *Hot cross buns* figure move by leaps or by steps? (leaps)
- How many times does it occur? (four)
- Where are all the places where the melody moves quickly by step? (bars 3, 6, 7 – they can answer by description or by putting up their hands in performance.)

Performing

Using tuned instruments teach the class to play *Hot cross buns*, first isolating the initial three notes:

and then the step-wise section:

Make sure that the children sing as they put the fragments together to make whole phrases. Once the piece can be played confidently at a moderate tempo, ask the children to think of ways by which it could be made more musically varied (e.g. by varying the dynamics between *forte* and *piano* for repeated fragments).

Suggest that the melody be divided, with metal instruments such as glockenspiels and chime bars used for the leaping movement and wooden instruments (xylophones) accentuating the contrast by playing the step-wise movement.

Untuned instruments could also be introduced for greater effect – a shaken tambourine, for example, or a vibrating triangle or vibraslap to heighten each of the long notes (i.e. on 'buns'). Perform and record on tape.

Assessment points

- ◆ How many of the class are able to perform both melodies with reasonable accuracy?
- ◆ How well do children show their understanding of the melodic shapes of each of the tunes?
- ◆ Do the children show imagination and sensitivity in making suggestions for changes of dynamics.

Stomping piece

Musical learning

Instrumental performance: tune and accompaniment; playing from notation

Structure: sensing the way the accompaniment supports the tune

Listening: Haydn and Carmines; listening and responding to the bass line; identifying an instrument (piano); noticing contrasts of style and articulation

DT

Performing

Teach the children to play the tune. You may wish to use this simple piano accompaniment to provide an initial supportive framework:

When they perform the tune sufficiently well in unison, practise with them the following accompaniment on alto and/or bass instruments:

Put the melody and accompaniment together. Take time to do this first as two halves of the class and then by further sub-dividing into small groups, providing the notation for each group. Ask some groups to practise section A and others to practise section B. Finally perform as a whole class.

Listening and appraising

Discuss the effect of putting the parts together. Draw attention to the lower part and its place in providing a supportive (bass) line for the melody.

In the following two extracts invite the class to demonstrate, by using their arms, if seated, or by movement if space allows, how they feel the lowest part moves:
- *Honky Tonk Train Blues* (Meade Lux Lewis)
- *Promenade: Walking the Dog* (Gershwin)

Lead the children to notice that, in the first extract, *Honky Tonk Train Blues*, there is one instrument only, the 'piano'. In the second, *Promenade: Walking the Dog*, it is a full orchestra.

Afterwards ask them to write down their ideas about the character and mood of the two extracts. The 'blues' piece has a 'stomping-like', relentless rhythmic quality. This contrasts with the more relaxed, carefree style of the orchestral piece.

Performing

Later, return to the performing activity. Encourage the children to apply the precise, rhythmic blues style to produce a faster performance of 'Stomping'. Alternatively, they might play the 'Stomping' piece slowly in a jaunty or carefree style and then discuss the overall effect.

Assessment points

- ◆ How adeptly do the children play the *Stomping piece* as an ensemble?
- ◆ Are they able to co-ordinate the performance of accompaniment and melody with reasonable ease?
- ◆ How well do the children show in movement their perception of the different lower parts?
- ◆ Does their movement, with its attention to character and mood, affect and improve the performing activity?
- ◆ Does their movement, with its attention to character and mood, affect and improve the final performing activity?

*Practising and
refining performing
skills*

*Expressing ideas
and opinions about
music and their
own performances*

*Refining interaction
and co-operation
within performing
groups*

Module review

Revise the *Om, pom, poddledum* song, giving turns to different groups of children to perform the least to the most demanding ostinato accompaniment.

Then ask the children to select their favourite pieces from this module. Organize them in groups of about six with the task of preparing a performance to present to each other.

After the initial performance of pieces, encourage the performers, as a group, to critically appraise their own work and suggest ways in which they could enhance it, for example, by improving their ensemble technique (timing, response), by varying their dynamics, by appointing one of the group as a conductor.

Arrange for further rehearsal time before presenting performances again and tape recording the results. Talk about what the children have learned from the module and encourage each one to write down what they have enjoyed learning most of all.

This would be an appropriate time to extend group self-assessment to individual self-assessment. In addition to stating what they have enjoyed learning, begin to develop simple self-assessment sheets to support your record-keeping. For example:

'I am confident that I can . . . '
'I feel I need more practice in . . . '

Assessment points

What have individual children achieved with respect to their performing skills:
◆ technical mastery of instruments and beaters?
◆ consolidating technical aspects of singing (posture, breathing, phrasing, articulation and intonation)
◆ timing and co-ordination?
◆ playing by ear?
◆ playing from notational cues?

*Refining
perceptions of pitch,
dynamics, duration*

*Improvising vocal
sounds, with
contrasts of pitch,
dynamics, duration*

*Notation and
improvisation:
interpreting graphic
scores in vocal
sounds*

*Composing:
structuring a
sequence of vocal
sounds*

*Refining vocal
improvisation skills
– incorporating
sounds into a song*

Voice-sounds

Improvising

Seated in a circle with the children, choose a vowel sound. Sing and sustain it. Question the children – was it high, medium or low? What else can they say about it? (very long, very quiet or very loud, for example)

Review all the vowel sounds, and then, as you did with the Name Game, go round the class individually, asking children to make a different sound from the previous one. It must be a different vowel and a contrasting pitch level, e.g. Leah sings 'e' at a high pitch level, Asif sings 'o' very low.

After several turns, check if the children remember who sang what, noting the different contributions.

Next, explore the effect of changing from low to medium to high pitch and back again while maintaining one vowel sound.

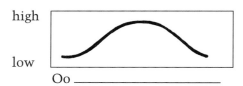

Ask children to work in pairs to practise together imitating and comparing sounds.

Interpreting symbols

Show the children the set of cards opposite. (Display the page or draw the images on the board.)

Using the first card, as an example, ask for someone's ideas as to how we could translate these symbols into sound. Start with a medium-pitched 'hum', gradually moving up and then down. Challenge individuals to interpret the other four cards similarly.

Composing

When the idea is fully grasped, equip children, in groups of five, with sets of these cards. (For this activity only, you may photocopy the images from the page opposite.) Give them a time limit and ask them to practise, rehearse and decide on a sequence which can be repeated three times. Eventually bring the children back as a class to share their results. Decide on a starting and stopping signal and record the items on tape cassette.

Applying vocal improvisation skills

Teach the children the following song, encouraging them individually to apply their skills in improvising vocally in the bars indicated. Provide a continuous tapped or finger-clicked pulse as a supportive framework if necessary.

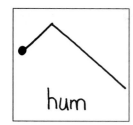   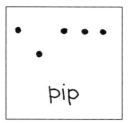 

Poppidee, poppidee, pop

Musical learning

Listening: Bartók; describing the music in terms of expression and atmosphere; discerning the musical techniques used, and their expressive effect

Exploring instruments and the types of sounds they make; learning how to control or modify the sounds; playing techniques

Improvising and composing from a dramatic/atmospheric stimulus; structuring ideas into a composition, employing contrasts; recording the composition as a graphic score

Instrument-sounds

Listening

Ask the children to listen carefully to an extract from the third movement of Bartók's *Music for Strings, Percussion and Celeste*, where the capabilities of stringed instruments are extended to create a very atmospheric piece of music. Afterwards ask:
- What words would describe this music? (likely answers: ghostly, creepy, haunted house)
- What made it sound like that?

Probe their understanding with further questions to tease out their response to the expressive effect of the music – slithery, sliding, etc. Then turn to recognizing different musical elements such as tempo, pitch, dynamic level.

Exploring instrumental sounds

Have already assembled in the centre of the room a set of beaters and a selection of instruments, clustered in two groups. For instance, group 1: tambourine, shaker, drum, cowbell, vibraslap, cymbal with beater, two-tone woodblock, claves; group 2: xylophone, chime bar, glockenspiel, metallophone, recorder.

Invite the children to test the instruments to find out which make short sounds (e.g. claves, woodblock, xylophone) and which make long sounds (e.g. beaten cymbal, metallophones, chime bar, recorder).

Divide the children into small groups to investigate either:
1 How they could shorten sounds on naturally sustaining metal instruments
2 How they could lengthen sounds on naturally non-sustaining instruments

After this, class discussion should reveal that a rapid two-beater tremolo (continuous alternating beaters on one note) gives a lengthening effect. Ways of shortening or dampening the sound on metal instruments are achieved by stopping the sound with the hand. Let the groups change over to experience both activities.

Creating atmospheric music

Ask the children to imagine that they are walking through a dark, thickly wooded forest. Get them to think about how they might walk, with individual children demonstrating tentative, cautious steps. Encourage vocabulary such as quietly walking, darkness, stillness, possibly using a favourite story as a stimulus, such as the first part of *The Minpins* by Roald Dahl.

Using a brass metallophone or alto glockenspiel, and reminding the children of the skills developed in Module 2, show how a 'walking part' could be improvised to match the steps of the 'walker'. Play a simple ostinato figure such as:

Encourage individuals to take turns to do the same, and build up a class improvisation where the sights and sounds of the forest are explored. Questions will need to be posed such as 'Is it daytime or is it night?' 'Which animals and birds might we hear?' 'Is it windy or is it still?' Then encourage the children's ideas with respect to trees, boughs creaking in the wind, twigs breaking underfoot and the cries and calls of forest creatures. Consider the many ideas presented by the children.

Encourage them to choose appropriate instruments and to experiment with the techniques already developed for extending the capabilities of instruments. In a class of thirty or so it may be necessary to pass round instruments so that all children have equal access to the activity.

Composing extension

Building up this activity, set a task for small groups of children to create a 'Sounds of the Forest' piece, using the idea of the walking ostinato part. They need to decide how to start and how to end, when to repeat and when to bring in contrasting ideas, with one child as a conductor bringing in the different parts according to their plan. Perform these in turn and ask the children to record them on large sheets of paper to display on the wall. You may wish to record the performances (audio or video).

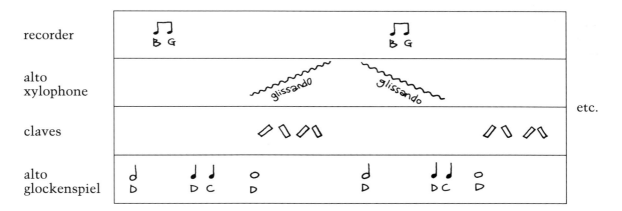

Encourage the class to ask each performing group questions about how they decided how to start, or how to end, how long to make it, and which ideas to use.

Assessment points

◆ In tackling the listening extract, were the children able to make informed comments about its mood and character (i.e. its expressiveness)?
◆ How responsively and responsibly did they explore, investigate and experiment with the instruments and their capabilities?
◆ How well did the groups progress in composing pieces which had:
a) clear structure (beginning, middle, end, use of repetition and contrast)
b) sensitivity in creating mood and atmosphere (choice of instruments/techniques, handling of musical concepts)

Free as the air

Musical learning

Composing to match the mood/atmosphere of a poem – choosing instruments and structuring sounds accordingly

Rehearsing, refining and performing their composition

Listening: Indian classical music; responding to mood through movement

Experimenting with instrumental effects

Composing

Ask the children to listen to this poem. Then ask individual children to read it aloud.

The Balloon

I felt free as the air as I left her hand,
Soaring, soaring way up high,
Into the wide, wide span of the sky
Towards the clouds and further 'til
I floated endlessly and the world stood still.

DT

Discuss how to approach the composing of a piece of music which could accompany this poem – music which would convey its feeling of lightness and weightlessness. Talk about the ideas presented by the poem concerning space, sky, clouds; and how we might choose instruments and space out sounds to communicate its feeling. Ideas to be encouraged include:

- conveying the feeling of space
- choosing specific effects from instruments
- light sounds
- movement of the balloon (low to high)
- spacing out the sounds

Structuring the piece

Organize the children into small groups. Suggest that they take time to explore ideas before rehearsing and refining them. At an interim stage share the groups' results and then give time to incorporate further ideas for improvement, before a final performance and recording.

Listening and responding

Play track 8 of the CD, an extract of Indian music featuring the Sarod – a stringed instrument which makes a rich, expressive sound. After listening once, ask the children, in pairs, to move in a way which shows the character and mood of the music.

Afterwards challenge the children to create a similar sound, experimenting with the strings of a violin or cello and with different size rubber bands stretched around boxes. Try the effect of experimenting with pieces of cardboard rapidly drawn back and forth beneath a beaten chime bar.

Assessment points

◆ Do the children respond appropriately to the poem by sensitively interpreting its feelings and mood in musical sound?

◆ Do children show an ability to achieve an intended effect, mood or atmosphere in their compositions?

◆ Notice the extent to which individual children's musical sensitivity and sense of timing is revealed through movement?

Speed, bonny boat

After some vocal warm-ups, teach the class the song (also known as the *Skye boat song*). Encourage legato singing which is energetic, accentuating the first beat of the bar and with good diction. Foster a well-sustained tone. Develop the children's ability to hold the long notes at the end of phrases. Get them to listen carefully to their singing and to suggest ways of improving it – e.g. make a difference in dynamic level to bring out the two phrases beginning 'Loud the winds howls', without forcing the tone. Enunciate words clearly.

Tap out the two rhythm patterns below. Ask which words of the song go with each pattern.

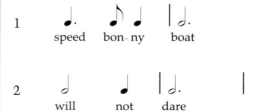

1   speed   bon- ny   boat

2   will   not   dare

38

Performing

Sing the song again, using each of the two patterns in turn as an ostinato accompaniment. Transfer the patterns to untuned percussion instruments with distinctively different sounds, asking the children to select the most appropriate instrument, taking particular care with example 2 which has two long notes to sustain.

Practise before adding them first separately and then together as an accompaniment to the song, small groups taking turns to play the accompanying ostinatos while the rest of the class sing.

Improvising

Ask everyone to put down their instruments and tap out the first bar of rhythm pattern 1 followed by the first bar of rhythm pattern 2 three times followed by a long note to finish.

Now, take a set of six chime bars: G A B C D E. While the children tap out the extended rhythm pattern, demonstrate how to improvise a melody to it, using the six notes. Here are two examples:

Ask a child to volunteer to make up another improvised tune using this pattern, while the class provides the rhythm framework as before.

Performing and appraising

Set out the chime bars in the centre of the circle. Taking the song at a slow speed, select individual children to improvise on the set of six notes, encouraging them to keep going first with an introduction and then with an interlude between verses of the song. Ask the class to tap out rhythm pattern 2 gently on their laps.

Record the performance and then play it back for appraisal by the class. What did you like about each of the improvisations? This should elicit comments to do with 'keeping going', 'playing a good tune', 'the way in which the bars were played', etc. Extend the activity to ensure that everyone has a turn to improvise.

Assessment points

◆ How quickly did the children apply their vocal skills with respect to learning the song?

◆ Were the children able to maintain their ostinato?

◆ Record the achievement of the children in improvising and in playing the ostinato introductions and interludes.

Call and response

Musical learning

Structure: call and response

Melody: awareness of a 'tonic' or 'home note', and its function within a song

Part-singing: separating into two groups for call-and-response performance

Composing a tune for a given text

Notation: recording their compositions using letter-names

Performing

Ask the class if they know the traditional song *There's a hole in my bucket*. Draw attention to its question and answer (or call and response) design, where the words differ but the music is basically the same:

Now introduce a traditional Jamaican song *Thread needle*. This has a similar construction with a short three-note answering phrase.

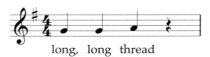

First teach the class to sing this three-note response pattern. Then sing the song through with the children inserting the response phrase as appropriate. Play the song to them, asking how many times the 'Long, long thread' patterns occur. Then teach them the whole song, drawing attention to the fact that the 'Long, long thread' pattern comes eight times before the final response phrase, which has a different final note:

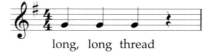

Now divide the class into two halves and get them to sing alternately – one half the call and one half the response. Change over. Experiment with different dynamic levels, e.g. quiet/quiet, loud/quiet, quiet/loud.

Alternatively, organize the children in pairs to clap the hands of their partners on 'Long, long, thread'.

Thread Needle

Jamaican Children's Song

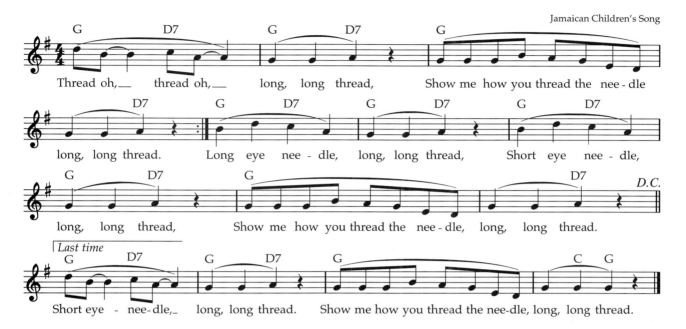

Thread oh,___ thread oh,___ long, long thread, Show me how you thread the nee-dle long, long thread. Long eye nee-dle, long, long thread, Short eye nee-dle, long, long thread, Show me how you thread the nee-dle, long, long thread.

Short eye - nee-dle,_ long, long thread. Show me how you thread the nee-dle, long, long thread.

Composing

Present the following word-play to the children, asking them to follow your call with the response 'Just like me'.

> I climbed a pair of stairs
> > Just like me
> I climbed two pairs of stairs
> > Just like me
> I went into a room
> > Just like me
> I looked out of a window
> > Just like me
> And then I saw a monkey
> > JUST LIKE ME

Now suggest that pairs of children, working at different times, set it to music in a similar way to *Thread needle*, using a set of six notes C D E F G A. As in *Thread needle*, the golden rule is that the response, 'Just like me' must not end on the home note 'C' until the very end. Some children might wish to use recorders, others their voices. Encourage them to use letter names to record their compositions. Subsequently share these performances, asking children to notice the interesting ways in which their friends have set the words. Display samples of work on the wall.

Assessment points

◆ How well do the children show their understanding of the call and response structure?

◆ How inventively do pairs of children carry out the composing task?

◆ Note the ability of pairs, when sharing their compositions with the rest of the class, to perform the task confidently.

41

Awakening (Review lesson)

Musical learning

Composing a collage – vocal and instrumental sounds – use of contrasts to provide structure and expression

Extension: use of Information and Communication Technology (ICT)

Remind the children of the experimental work that they did with instruments previously, extending their capabilities to lengthen and shorten sounds.

In groups of six, ask the children to imagine that they are composing a collage of contrasting vocal (half the group) and instrumental sounds (half the group), based on the idea of 'The city starts to wake up'. Check progress by occasionally asking groups to show everyone how far they have got.

At stages, ask the children to think about how they will decide how lightly or how heavily to sing or play – encouraging controlled contrasts of quiet and loud sounds. Similarly, get them to think about contrasting low with high, moving from low to high, fast and slow.

Introduce opportunities for individual children to include fragments of melodies on alto glockenspiels, metallophones, chime bars or recorders at appropriate points in the composition. Point out that interspersing melodic fragments can help to give structure to a piece – the vocal and instrumental sounds in free time contrast with structured melodic aspects.

Discuss each group's efforts and record them on audio and/or video tape.

Extension

Can the children think of ways to develop this idea as a class activity by tape recording 'environmental' city sounds (e.g. traffic, squealing tyres, aeroplanes, telephones, etc.) to intersperse into their compositions, in this way developing their work further?

Assessment points

How well have the children's skills developed with respect to:
- vocal improvisation and composition?
- instrumental improvisation and composition?
- originality of ideas?
- sensitivity to musical concepts and expression?
- imaginatively exploring and using environmental sounds?

Introducing rhythmic notation

**Musical
learning**

*Notation: inventing
graphic notation to
convey durations –
long and short
sounds; following
such notation while
listening;
performing from
such notation*

Listening: Susato

*Composing:
structuring a
combination of
different ostinatos*

*Performing: playing
and conducting the
ostinatos
composition*

Through the course of this module, notation of rhythm and pitch are
introduced, first through graphic notation of duration, and then pitch,
moving into conventional notation in subsequent lessons.

*Remember that the length of a note is a relative concept: a long note is only
so in relation to a short one. In this module you will encounter crotchets and
quavers. Interpret the crotchets as long notes and the quavers as short ones.*

First, ask your class to notate the following example by drawing marks
which represent the length (or duration) of the sounds they hear. Sing or play
three long notes to your class as shown below. Make sure the rest is equal to
the length of note played.

The marks they make might look something like this:

A straight line is the simplest way to represent each round, but other
solutions may be just as 'correct', for instance:

Encourage the class to notate the silences between notes as accurately as
they notate the sounds. Ask your class the following questions:
* how long is the note? (in seconds);
* how long is the silence (or rest)?

Now sing or play a series of short sounds. Again, play the rests as equal
values to the notes.

As before, ask your class to notate what they have heard, listening carefully
to the lengths of the notes and the lengths of the rests (or gaps). The outcome
could be something like this:

— — — — — — — — — — — —

or possibly something like this:

· · · · · · · · · · · · · · ·

Now play this rhythm – a combination of long and short durations:

long   short short   long   short short   long   short short   *etc.*

Invite your class to notate this combination of long and short sounds using the notation they have already devised. Examples are given below.

or

 9 Now listen to an extract from Susato's 'La mourisque'. What does your class notice about the rhythm of this piece? (It stays the same throughout; it's an ostinato.) Ask them to perform the rhythm along with the recording, and then to follow their notation of the rhythm, following the shape with their fingers.

Split your class into groups. Ask each group to perform one of the six notations (below) as an ostinato. Various different sounds could be used, for instance:

- finger clicks
- slap thighs
- clapping hands
- rubbing hands

Performing

Ask a child to conduct the whole class, inviting all the groups to play the ostinatos together or separately.

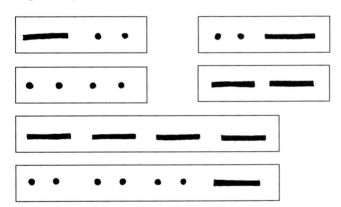

There will be many different ways in which the ostinatos can be combined. Explore some formal designs which give the rhythms a shape or pattern.

Assessment points

- ◆ Were they able accurately to trace the relative durations and silences?
- ◆ Were they able to interpret accurately the graphic notation?
- ◆ Were they able to be precise rhythmically about performing note values?
- ◆ Were individuals able to piece together a structure and were the groups able to perform their rhythms accurately with a feeling for ensemble?

The Padstow song

Teach your class *The Padstow song,* with appropriate references to breathing, posture, dynamics, phrasing and so forth.

When they have learned the song, divide the class into two groups: one group will be singers and the other will clap or play rhythms in four smaller sub-groups.

Trad. arr. DT/WRM

2. The young boys of Padstow,
   They might if they would,
   For summer is a-coming today.
   They might have made a ship
   and gilded it with gold,
   In the merry morning of May.

46

3. The young girls of Padstow,
   They might if they would,
   For summer is a-coming today.
   They might have made a garland
   Of roses white and red,
   In the merry morning of May.

4. O where are the young men,
   That now would have danced,
   For summer is a-coming today.
   O some they are in England
   And some they are in France
   In the merry morning of May.

Ask your class to listen to, and then write down, the rhythms of the left-hand part of the piano accompaniment.

Make the following cards and hand them out to the four sub-groups.

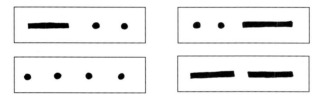

Each sub-group plays their rhythm as an ostinato. Start the ostinatos first, then add the music. Use the following structure, which you could write on the board to help the class:

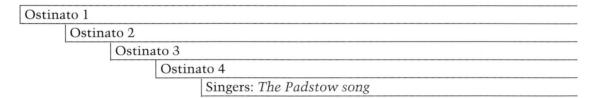

Each group adds their ostinato in turn, and all may be conducted by one of the class, who can bring in each group at his or her own choice, creating a new structure.

When this principle has been mastered, change the singers and ostinato players over, so that those clapping or playing the ostinatos now have the chance to sing the *Padstow song*.

Assessment points

◆ Were the clapping groups able to perform and maintain their ostinato from the card?
◆ Was each group able to hold its own when other ostinato rhythms were added by other groups?
◆ Were they able to read the graphic notation precisely?
◆ Were they able to be precise rhythmically about performing note values from the cards?

Musical learning

Pitch: awareness of high, medium, low; refining ability to describe sounds in pitch and duration

Notation: developing and using graphic notation to describe pitch as well as duration; playing from such notation; graphically notating a known tune

Introducing pitch notation

Make a variety of high- and low-pitched sounds to your class. Here are a few examples:
- high guitar or piano notes
- low guitar or piano notes
- a bass drum
- the top note of a soprano glockenspiel

Ask your class to shut their eyes and listen to these sounds and other sounds around them in the school. Ask them to describe what they hear. From these sounds, draw up a list on the board, differentiating between high- and low-pitched sounds.

The children may notice that on some instruments the lower notes sustain for longer than the higher ones. Can they use words to describe these sounds? Some examples might be:

high	medium	low
thin	half way	fat
light	mid way	heavy
tinkling	average	deep
shrill	middling	growly
little	between	big

Can they find a way of representing these notes on a piece of paper?

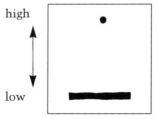

Encourage your class to find a notation to describe sounds in pitch and duration. Ask the children to use their hands to help them to describe what they hear:
- high and short notes
- low and long notes
- medium-pitched notes, long or short

Notate the graph on the opposite page on the board, and ask individual children to play what they see on a piano or a tuned percussion instrument.

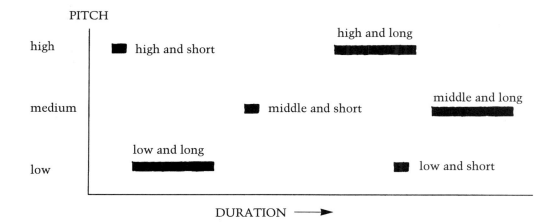

Play the tune *Hot cross buns* to your class (see Module 2 Lesson 4). Ask your class to try to notate the pitches shown below in a graphic form.

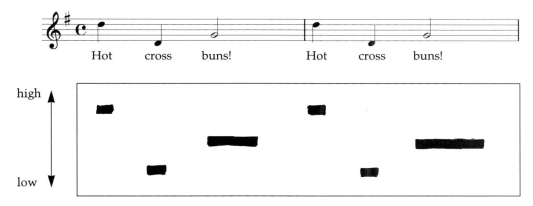

You might have to play the fragment several times, so that your class can have an opportunity to notate their symbols; then continue with the rest of the tune, and ask the class to try to write it down.

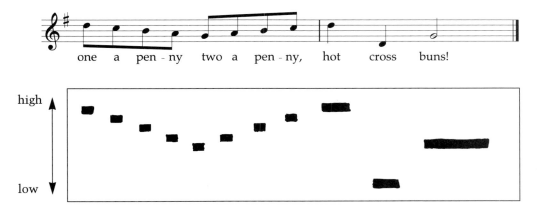

Assessment points

◆ How easily do the children distinguish between high, medium and low pitches from a variety of sound sources?
◆ Were your class able to develop and use a concise graphic notation for short and long low-, medium- and high-pitched sounds?
◆ Were they able to use their notation with confidence to express what they heard?

Notating rhythms

Remind your class of long and short note values. You may like to link this with the left hand part of the *Padstow song*. Now show your class these notations of long and short note values:

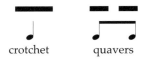

crotchet   quavers

Link the value of the crotchet with the symbol ▬▬ (long) and the quaver with ▬ (short), as used earlier in this module. Explain to the class that this is how musicians write down and read their music.

Show your class a score of a piece of music and ask them what they see. Some obvious signs and symbols will be dynamic markings, tempo markings, phrase marks, crotchets and quavers and so forth.

Point out to your group that each note has a head and a stem and ask them to have a go at drawing them for themselves.

When several quavers are written together, the stems are joined by beams, rather like people linking their arms together across their shoulders, as Greek dancers do.

When a quaver occurs on its own, it has a distinctive tail; it looks as if it has an arm which hangs down by its side.

Explain to your class that the time-value of a crotchet is twice that of a quaver. Two quavers equal one crotchet.

Now re-introduce the Name Game (module 1 lesson 2). The basis of the material here is fundamentally an extension of that game, except that now the object is to write down the note values that the children hear, and perform them using the information learned in earlier lessons in this module.

Ask a child to repeat a particular name that has an uncomplicated rhythm (for example, a name that contains only one syllable – Paul, or Joe), and split this short rhythmic phrase into two parts. For example:

Does the class notice the rests after 'Paul'?

You could ask the class to analyse the two parts using the following questions:

In the first part, 'my name is':
- are the note values equal or unequal? (equal)
- are the note values long or short? (long)
- what note values are the class going to assign to the three words 'my name is'? (crotchets)
- do the notes have one count or 'beat' each? (yes)

In the second part (the name):
- is the rhythm of 'Paul' the same (or different) to the words in part 1 'my' or 'name' or 'is'? (the same)
- what rhythmic value is assigned to this note? (a crotchet)

Bar-lines

Introduce an accent or a stress to the word 'Paul' in the last example. Tell your class that they can add a bar-line to divide part 1 from part 2. It is not important for the present to discuss time signatures – the concept of a bar-line is introduced to show where emphasis falls.

Once the class has built up an example of a name (with a bar-line) on the blackboard, using the components of the rhythm (parts 1 and 2), the following rhythms might be tackled, using the same formula as above.

a series of 5 crotchets

Ask your class to show where the accent falls, on each name, by placing the bar-line in front of the accented syllable.

3 crotchets and two quavers   3 crotchets, two quavers and a crotchet

an example where part 1 includes two quavers   3 crotchets, a crotchet and two quavers

My   name   is E - liz - a beth   My   name   is   Rose - ma-ry
            part 1   *part 2*   *part 1*   *part 2*

Notating and performing

Divide the class into four or five groups and ask each group to write down the names of each person in the group onto a card, using crotchets and quavers to show long and short notes.

When this has been done, each group should perform their cards.

Assessment points

◆ Were they able to distinguish same-value syllables from shorter durations?
◆ Did they understand that some notes have the same value ('my name is'), whilst some are faster ('An – tho – ny')?
◆ Were the children in groups able to produce a fluent performance of the names?
◆ Did they practise this sufficiently?

Musical learning

Notation: progressing from graphic notation of high and low pitch to introducing the 5-line staff and the treble (G) clef; practising drawing the treble clef

Introducing the five-line staff

Making the giant leap from improvising, composing and performing music – either by ear or from graphic notation – to working from pitch notation can be a complex task.

In the notation of music, either through conventional notation or graphic score, there are two elements to be considered:

In Lesson 2 the horizontal aspect (duration) was considered in some detail, now attention is turned to the vertical element, pitch.

In Lesson 2 the notation of high- medium- and low-pitched sounds was introduced. If the 'high' and 'low' is more finely graded, we have the basis of the musical staff. A more sophisticated, graded axis can be used, with three lines and two spaces.

High

Middle

Low

Now it is possible to develop this graph into something which looks more like a musical staff. Explain to your class that in this more finely-graded diagram there are five lines and four spaces:

Higher still
Higher
Middle
Lower
Lower still

Now the staff needs to have a fixed point of reference to say where a particular note or pitch belongs. We will use the *treble clef*. The centre of the clef, from where we begin to draw, is on the second line up from the bottom, and fixes the note known as G.

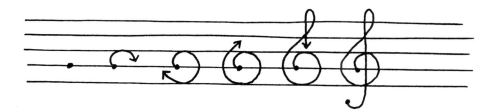

This might be a good moment for you to move from illustrating on the board to inviting the class to begin to write these things down for themselves on paper. Ask your children to draw the music lines and add a treble clef. Much fun can be had with this artistic aspect of musical notation. The class should be encouraged to spend some time drawing the staff using a ruler, remembering the following:

- The staff has five lines and four spaces.
- Bar-lines touch the bottom and top of the staff.
- A piece ends with a double bar-line.
- The treble clef starts on the second line up, known as G.

Ask your class to practise drawing the lines of the staff and a treble clef. On the completed lines they should add the note G.

Assessment points

◆ Were the children able to draw the lines and a treble clef?
◆ Does your class understand that G is a fixed point on the staff where the treble clef begins?
◆ Do they understand that the staff has five lines and four spaces?

B A G

Having established the location of G on the staff, tell your class that the note in the next space above is A. Use note heads only, to focus the children's attention on the lines and spaces, which fix the positions of G and A. Ask your class to draw these notes on the staff and clef they have drawn in the last lesson.

G   A   G   A

Having established G and A, introduce the note B, which sits on the middle line of the staff.

B   A   G

Now give your class some manuscript paper. The five lines should be widely spaced to allow the class to draw the notes on the staff.

Invite some of your children to play these three notes on a tuned percussion instrument. Can the class identify any pieces of music which begin with these three notes?

Point out to your group that they can spell the word B A G using these three notes, and that they also form the first three notes of *Three blind mice*.

Turn these notes upside down, and it will give the first notes of *Frère Jacques*.

G   A   B   G

Composing

Can the class or groups compose, write down and perform their own three-note tune (repeating notes as required) and perform it on tuned percussion or recorders?

Listening

Play the first section of 'Carillon' from Bizet's *L'Arlésienne*, Suite No.1. Can the class put these three notes into the correct order to give the notation for the bells in this piece? Ask your children to trace the notes on their manuscript paper as they are played.

B   G   A   B   G   A

Musical learning

Notation: learning the notes G A B; relating the notation to the sound; practising writing in staff notation

Listening: Bizet – notating a repeated pattern from the extract

Learning to play and sing a 3-note tune from notation; performing it with tuned and untuned percussion accompaniment

Now teach your class the following three-note folk tune. It is a Hungarian melody and was originally collected by Béla Bartók. The objective in this lesson is to learn to sing the tune from notation – by writing it out, naming the notes, and clapping and tapping the rhythms. The children should get to know the note letter-names, and read the notes on the staff. The class should also aim to play the piece on tuned percussion, applying the techniques learned in Module 2.

Clip-clop

Invite your class to use their hands to show whether the notes are high, medium or low in pitch. They could do this as they sing the tune to 'la' or as you play it.

Some children might add the bass part using a bass xylophone. Others might add a horse-like percussion part using temple blocks or claves.

When the piece has been learned it can be performed to another class or at assembly.

Assessment points

◆ Were they able to make the relationship between G on the second line and A in the space above?
◆ Can they put the three notes in the correct order for the Bizet extract and trace the notes with a finger?
◆ How much attention is your class putting on reading the notation?
◆ Were they able to write out the music?
◆ Were your class able to name the notes of the tune?
◆ When performing the piece, did they practise enough? Did they read the music?
◆ Were they able to co-ordinate an ensemble performance and stay together?
◆ Were they able to clap and tap the rhythms of notes?

Verse and chorus

Listening and appraising

Ask your class to listen to the song *Rule, Britannia!* by the 18th-century composer Thomas Arne. This song is often associated with the Last Night of the Proms. If you have a video of this event, show it to your class.

Ask your class what they notice about the music:

- How often does the soprano soloist sing?
- When do the choir and audience begin to sing?
- What words do the choir and audience sing?
- Does the soloist sing the same words each time?

Point out that the music is structured in such a way that the soprano soloist sings a verse and then the choir and audience sing the chorus. Ask your class to help you compile a list of features relating to the verse and the chorus, for example:

verse
- soloist alone
- orchestra accompanies the soprano soloist
- moderately loud singing

chorus
- soloist is joined by the choir and audience
- the volume gets louder

At the Last Night of the Proms the audience have flags and banners, and when the chorus begins they all join in and wave their flags and banners high in the air. Possibly your children could make flags – of any nationality – and wave them during the chorus, to help distinguish it from the verse.

Teach your children the chorus only, and play the CD. When the chorus begins they can join in. Don't forget to sing in phrases; take a good breath.

Teach your class another song with a strong verse-chorus structure, *Donkey riding.* This was a Canadian song sung by lumbermen.

Musical learning

Listening: Arne

Structure: verse and chorus; using this terminology

Performing verse-and-chorus songs, with awareness of structure

Donkey riding

2. Were you ever in Cardiff Bay,
   Where the folks all shout 'Hooray!'
   Here comes John with his three months' pay,
   Riding on a donkey?'

Hey-ho! Away we go,
Donkey riding, donkey riding,
Hey-ho! Away we go,
Riding on a donkey.

Performing

Divide your class into two groups. These could be of equal size, or use a handful of good singers to sing the verse and the rest of the class to sing the chorus.

Assessment points

◆ Are the children able to use the technical words introduced in this lesson with confidence? (soprano, verse, chorus)
◆ Was the group able to distinguish between the verse and the chorus and anticipate where the chorus begins?

*Listening: Dukas;
describing the piece
in musical terms;
relating it to a story*

*Performing
(acting/mime/
dance): enacting a
story, partly of their
own devising, to a
given music
soundtrack; aiming
closely to match
the music in mood
and movement;
constructive
evaluation of other
groups'
performances*

*Cross-curricular
links*

Drama

The Sorcerer's Apprentice

Without explanation, begin reading the following to your class:
Imagine that you are in a wizard's workshop. It is a place full of bottles and
jars. Bottles with nasty green slime, or dried pigeons' eyes; jars with bats'
wings or toads' legs. Vats of dried leaves or secret juices for making
concoctions and spells. There are so many bottles on the tall shelves that
you cannot possibly begin to count them all.

In the middle of the room is a cauldron, a steaming pot with a rather nasty
smell. The Wizard is teaching you how to make a remedy for a bad foot. He
has told you never, ever, under any circumstances, to open one particular
bottle high up on a shelf, well out of reach. But now the Wizard has gone out
and left you to stir the cauldron. Your curiosity gets the better of you.
Standing on a box, you fumble for the bottle he has told you never to touch.
You open it. Nothing happens. So you tip just a little, tiny helping into his
steaming mixture. Nothing happens – not at first. But slowly, something
begins to bubble in the cauldron, something ominous is happening. He told
you never to open the bottle. And now you have. Now you wish you'd never
opened it . . .

Ask your class to build up a set of words which best describe what is
happening above. Here are some examples:
- smelly
- creepy
- bubbly
- hot

Build up a list on the board of the words they would use to describe the
scene. Imagine the apprentice gazing into the cauldron as the special liquid
begins to bubble into action.

Now play your class the extract from Paul Dukas's *The Sorcerer's
Apprentice.*

Ask your class to build up a description of the music. For instance:
- It stops and starts.
- It is low in pitch.
- It sounds like a dance.
- It gets louder as it develops.

Any more?

Performing

Now split your class into several groups. They are going to enact the scene
described above. The cast should include the wizard, the apprentice, and
some of the objects in the workshop – which become animated as the music
builds up.
This scene falls into two parts:
- the part of the story they have already heard;
- the part of the story that they have to imagine.

The words the class collected to describe the scene, and their description of the music, will be of use to them in formulating the rest of their story.

- What happens when the wizard leaves the room?
- Does the mixture boil over the sides?
- How does the stop-and-start feature of the music relate to what happens in the mixture?
- What happens when the Wizard comes back into the room?

When the groups have prepared their story, play the music and allow them to perform to the other members of the class. The extract on the *Targeting Music* CD goes with the second part of the story – starting when the apprentice adds the mixture to the cauldron – but you may wish to use a longer extract from *The Sorcerer's Apprentice*; recordings are widely available.

Ask the children to evaluate each group's interpretation. If possible, use a video camera to record the performances.

Assessment points

◆ Were the class able constructively to evaluate each performance?
◆ Were their actions well matched to the music?
◆ Did their story build up to reflect the music's increase in excitement?
◆ Were they better at enacting the part of the story that they had read to them, or the part they had to improvise?

Musical learning

Listening: Renaissance Venetian music; understanding its historical context and purpose

Performing (acting/mime): enacting a coronation; matching the music in mood and movement

Instruments: understanding playing-styles through mime

Cross-curricular links

History, geography, drama

A Venetian coronation

Ask your class: what is a coronation? It is a ceremony surrounding the crowning of a king or queen.

Now show your class where Venice is on a map. Tell them that it is a city with canals instead of main roads; transport is by means of boats called gondolas. It is a port, and an important city in history.

Introduce your class to the word *Doge*. In the high renaissance in Venice this was a very important person – a chief magistrate, with his own sumptuous palace. Show your class both the picture of the Doge's Palace by Canaletto reproduced opposite, and Bellini's famous painting (below) of Doge Leonardo Loredan, which hangs in the National Gallery in London. Ask them to look at his hat (the ducal *beretta*), his stern and serious look – the look of a man who has much to do to look after his city. Ask them, too, to note how rich and fine his robes are.

Detail from *The Doge Leonardo Loredan* by Giovanni Bellini
© National Gallery, London

Music for special events

Help your class to understand that music from older periods was often written for special events.

Ask the class to think of occasions on which a composer might write music specifically for a great event:
- a great religious service
- a great royal occasion, such as a birthday or anniversary
- the state visit of a foreign guest

Preparing for performance

Ask your class to listen to the brief extracts on tracks 12–15 of the CD: the sounds of a Venetian Doge's coronation, around 1600. They are going to enact this great ceremony. (You may wish to do this as a whole class, or divided into a few large groups.)

Ask the class to imagine what the scene would be like; the great church of St Mark's, next to the Doge's palace, with a large piazza in front, filled with cheering crowds.

The cast should include:

The Doge	–	a pompous aristocratic figure
His attendants	–	who carry him around and look after him
His musicians	–	who play a variety of instruments including trumpets and drums
The crowds	–	who cheer him on

Props are not essential, but would help create the atmosphere:
- gowns and cloaks in festive colours – old curtains might be suitable
- representations of musical instruments: trumpets and stringed instruments
- the ducal beretta – not a heavy, jewelled crown, but rather a fancy pork-pie type of hat

Performing

As the class or groups hear the music they should try to fit specific events to each extract, so that they can build up a story line. Details of the extracts are given below, together with suggestions of what each extract might represent.

Ask the children what they notice about the music, its style and instrumentation. Try to help the children in this matter, as their musical perception will affect what they do.

Bells ringing
When the Doge was elected the bells would be rung around the city to celebrate. The children might enact the ringing of the bells.

Note that the bell is heavy and has a deep tone; it is rung slowly and solemnly with a deliberate rhythm.

Trumpets and drums arriving
The Doge arrives at the great church of St Mark's.

The drums are heard a long way away, and gradually get nearer. A great celebration begins. The drummers and trumpeters walk in a dignified procession, behind which follow the Doge and his attendants.

The drums are large and heavy and are played with two sticks. The trumpets are held high and may carry pendants.

The coronation
The Doge is crowned with a special hat known as the ducal *beretta*. Then he solemnly stands up, and his attendants and the crowd bow before him.

The musicians play different instruments now. What kind of instruments? Will they stand or sit to play them? Some are blown and some are bowed.

A Fanfare
The Doge might be presented to the people and carried round the piazza outside, throwing coins (minted specially for the occasion) to the excited assembled crowd. The trumpeters and drummers play again.

Extension

There is much scope here for extending the scene and adding text:
- Can the groups develop the story and link the scenes together into a more continuous whole?
- Can the groups write some dialogue?
- What are the names of the characters?
- Who are they?
- Where in Venice do they live?
- Will he be a good Doge?
- Better than the last one?
- Will he shower the people with gifts and presents like the last one did?

Assessment points

◆ Were the groups able effectively to match their drama to the music?
◆ How well did their acting suit the noble mood of the music?
◆ Was the dignity of the occasion clearly presented?
◆ Were the festivities represented?
◆ Were they able to characterize the playing of the trumpets and drums with conviction?

Musical learning

Instruments: identifying by appearance, by sound, by description and by knowledge of how the sounds are made; understanding instrument 'families'; learning about playing techniques

Listening: traditional, Stanley, Satie, Paganini

Extension: drawing an instrument; describing its sound in musical terms

Musical instruments

This lesson focuses on four particular instruments, but relates them to their respective 'families'. Lesson 5 extends the theme by focusing on some characteristic instrumental ensembles.

Divide your class into pairs or small groups. Photocopy the page opposite, and give a copy to each group. By looking at the pictures – but also by listening to the CD extracts, and to your descriptions of the construction and playing method – the groups should try to identify and name the instruments they see.

Woodwind family
These instruments are blown to make a sound. Most of them, but not all, are made of wood. Most have 'keys' which change the pitch by covering or uncovering holes, and which are played by the fingers. This music is 'Away in a Manger', played on two descant recorders.

Brass instruments
A family of instruments made of brass. Each instrument consists basically of a length of tube coiled up into a distinctive shape and blown with a mouthpiece. All these instruments have a flared end known as a 'bell'. This music is a Voluntary by John Stanley, played on a trumpet.

Keyboard instruments
When the keys of a piano are pressed, felt-covered hammers strike the strings to produce sounds. This music is *Gymnopédie No.1* by Erik Satie, played on a piano.

Stringed instruments
The strings are made to sound using a bow held in the right hand. The left hand presses down the strings in different places to change the pitch. Sometimes the strings may be plucked instead of using the bow. This music is from *Caprice No. 13* by Paganini, played on a violin.

When everyone has heard the extracts, ask the children to help you devise a list of words which describe each instrument.

Extension
Ask the children to draw a picture of one of the instruments which they remember most clearly. Underneath the picture they should include a description of what the instrument both *looks* like and *sounds* like.
- Was the sound soft or loud? (*forte* or *piano*)
- piercing or soothing?
- legato or staccato?
- bowed or pizzicato
- high or low in pitch
- which family of instruments does it belong to?

Build up a list of words which describe the sounds and the instruments.

Assessment points

◆ Could the children identify the instruments?
◆ Did they understand which instrument belonged to which family?
◆ Were the children able to identify the characteristics of their chosen instrument's sounds as listed in the extension above?
◆ Did their diagram include some technical aspects of the instruments?

Instrumental ensembles

Musical learning

Instruments: learning about various characteristic combinations of instruments; matching recorded extracts with pictures and descriptions; learning more about how the sounds are made

Terminology and musical elements: describing the sounds and styles heard

This lesson is an extension of Lesson 4; the instruments here are grouped in ensembles.

Play the four recordings. The children should think about the sounds they hear. Working as a class or in groups, ask them to build up a description in words:
- Are the sounds soft or loud?
- piercing or soothing?
- legato or staccato?
- bowed or pizzicato
- which family do the instruments belong to?

Display the opposite page, or photocopy it for handing out. Listen to the extracts again, and ask them to match their description with the picture.

Especially if working in groups, you could build up a collage of pictures and descriptions. Ask the children to add text to the collage, describing the instruments and how they are played.

Big band

A group of instruments that includes trumpets, trombones, saxophones, clarinets and drum kit. All these instruments, with the exception of the drums, are blown to produce sounds and are usually made of brass, except clarinets, which are usually made of wood.

Recorder ensemble

A group of small instruments usually made of wood, which are blown to produce sounds. The fingers of both hands are used to change the notes. The instruments are made in a variety of sizes.

String quartet

A group of stringed instruments: two violins, viola and cello. The violins and viola are held under the chin and all may either be played using a bow held in the right hand or by plucking the strings using the fingers of the same hand.

Pop group

This group consists of:
- electric guitar
- drum kit
- a singer
- a bass guitar

sometimes a group such as this may include an electronic keyboard.

How are the sounds produced from each instrument?

Assessment points

◆ Could the children match the recordings to the pictures?
◆ Can they identify the instrument in the picture by name?
◆ Do they understand how the sounds are produced?

Revision lesson

Musical learning

Revision

Describing feelings (likes and dislikes) about a piece of music or instrumental sound

Cross-curricular links

Language

To prepare, ask children to bring in a recording of their favourite music or instrument.

Go back over the material covered in this module, picking up especially on material that they particularly enjoyed. Play the CD extracts again and remind them of some of the topics covered, asking them to recall information about the music, instruments, mood and so forth.
- Verse–chorus structure, using *Rule Britannia!* and *Donkey riding*
- The *Sorcerer's Apprentice* by Dukas
- The coronation of the Doge
- Instruments; instrument families and groups

Ask some of your class to play a short extract from music they particularly like or an instrument they enjoy. Ask them to be critics of what they heard.

They should imagine that they are writing a review for a newspaper or a magazine to describe some of the music they have heard, and to pass on some enthusiasm for what they like about it. Can they provide a picture of their favourite instrument?

Alternatively, they may describe what it is about a particular sound or instrument that they dislike.

Assessment points

◆ For each of the music examples or extracts, analyse what your group liked or disliked. Why was this so?
◆ How well do their newspaper reviews reveal what they absorbed from the module?

Cinderella

a musical operetta by Margaret Rolf

Suggestions for classwork across a half-term

Everyone should be involved in learning the vocal parts, with maximum opportunities to sing, speak, play and dance – in groups, pairs or as an individual, as appropriate. When it comes to the performance, be flexible as to whether solo parts are actually sung solo or by a number of singers; a spoken solo part is not usually problematic.

Spread the work across six weeks in a progressive way to ensure that an eventual performance to other classes or to parents will evolve as a result of good classwork, unforced by performance pressure.
Suggestions: week 1 – songs 1 to 3
week 2 – songs 4 to 6
week 3 – song 7 and the Dance
week 4 – songs 8 and 9
week 5 – songs 10 and 11

Take a different focus each week even though new material will be being tackled, for instance as follows:

Week 1: learning good habits

Vocal warm-ups as advocated in Module 1, remembering good posture, head and shoulders relaxed, sitting up straight, slow, deep breathing. Teach the songs either unaccompanied or with the lightest of piano accompaniments. It is important right from the start to get the feel for the musical character of the material – see the accompanying notes on performing the songs. Remind the children of the need to **breathe** through the phrase, of good **intonation**, with well pronounced words, **vitality and attack** (initial consonants and letter blends).

Week 2: learning material

While continuing to learn the songs ensure that good habits are applied also to the quality of instrumental work. Ensure that instrumentalists are positioned comfortably with tuned instruments, at an appropriate height. Players should be able to see each other and the singers easily, preferably arranged in a circle. This will help timing and co-ordination. Care should be taken to balance the instruments with the singers, emphasizing that much of the work is accompanying except for places where there are special effects.

Week 3: practising

At this point the music already learned will be becoming known to the extent that the class will be 'getting it together', listening to each other, offering opportunities for different pupils and small groups to try out the solo parts. Rehearsing in a larger space will show everyone how we need to adapt and adjust to different locations, getting used to working flexibly to try out different effects.

Week 4: memorizing

By now the sharing of responsibilities between singers, instrumentalists, actors and narrators will be settling. At this stage a start will be made with memorizing, although much of the material will have been absorbed naturally.

Week 5: refining

In working on and refining *Cinderella* there will be a need to concentrate on the dramatic elements of the work, such as dramatic gestures to convey the meanings of the text, projecting and presenting to an audience, working on the dance.

Week 6: staging

The focus will now be on working within the chosen space, usually the school hall.
Time will be taken to check on movements across the space, where props will be situated, and where exits and entries will be made. The simplest of scenery, props, costumes and masks are often the most effective in conveying what is one of the most well known traditional stories.

Cinderella

Characters:
Narrator
Cinderella
Stepmother
2 Step-sisters
Messenger
Fairy Godmother
3 Rats
2 Footmen
Prince
Town Crier
King & Queen (optional – non-speaking)
Dancers (2 girls and 2 boys, to speak)
Chorus

Instruments:
Triangle
Claves
Tambourine
Cymbal
Drum
Scraper/Guiro
Coconut shells or temple blocks
Glockenspiels
Xylophones
Piano – adult

Scenery and Properties:
1. The kitchen
   Firewood
   Litter (paper, etc.)
   Pumpkin
   Invitation
   Brush
   Wand
   Various dresses, shoes, gloves, etc.
   Wrap

2. The Palace Ballroom
   Trays of food
   Small stool and cushion for shoe

Words and Music by Margaret Rolf. Performance notes (given in boxes) by Dorothy Taylor

Scene 1 – The Kitchen in Cinderella's House

STEPMOTHER   Cinderella!
(pause, stepmother and 2 sisters enter)

Cinderella! Where is that girl?
(sees Cinderella)

Oh! There you are. Have you made the beds?

CINDERELLA   *(cheerfully)* Yes, stepmother.

STEPMOTHER   Did you fetch the wood for the fire?

CINDERELLA   Yes, stepmother.

STEPMOTHER   Well, don't just sit around girl. Sweep this floor.

CINDERELLA   I have swept the floor, stepmother.

SISTER 1   Well, it's still dirty.
(Goes to fireplace, picks up sticks and drops them on to the floor)

You had better do it again.

SISTER 2   Yes, it's still very dirty.
(Drops more litter on the floor)

You'd better do it again, then you can prepare the dinner.
(Cinderella sweeps)

70

1. Wouldn't the world be lovely? (Cinderella and Chorus)

Margaret Rolf

1. What makes people mean and selfish?
    What makes people so unkind?
    Do they learn it from each other?
    Do they think that I don't mind?

    Wouldn't the world be lovely
    If ev'ryone was good?
    Wouldn't the world be beautiful
    If we did the things we should?
    But ev'ryone is different
    We all have good days and bad.
    But wouldn't the world be beautiful
    If nobody was sad?

2. What makes people grow so haughty?
    What makes other people cruel?
    Do they learn it from each other?
    They don't learn it at their school.

    Wouldn't the world be lovely . . .

Performance notes

Verse: good attack on consonants, clear words, detached notes, sung in an almost conspiratorial whisper. Breathe after 'selfish', 'unkind'.

Chorus: changes into compound time, change of mood suggests legato (smooth, gliding, expansive) singing. Sing through the long phrases in one breath, e.g. 'Wouldn't the world be lovely if everyone was good?'

NARRATOR   Cinderella lived with her two sisters in a house near the King's Palace. She was a kind and loving girl but her two sisters were cruel and proud. They were jealous of Cinderella's beauty and gentle ways. They were just like their mother, who had married Cinderella's father after his first wife had died. Cinderella was made to do all the work, while her two step-sisters admired themselves in their elegant dresses and jewels. When her work was done, she would go and sit among the cinders to keep warm. That is why she was called Cinderella.

Percussion accompaniment (*Wouldn't the world be lovely?*)

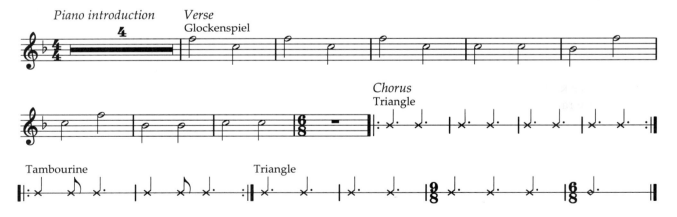

2. We have elegant dresses (Stepsisters and Chorus)

Margaret Rolf

1. We have elegant dresses,
    We have the richest jewels
    And we know that sometimes
    We are rather cruel, but –

    However much we nag,
    However much we scold,
    At the end of the day
    The truth must be told.
    She's the one who is happy,
    We're the ones who feel mad.

2. We have comfortable bedrooms,
    We have the tasty food
    And we know that sometimes
    We are rather rude, but –

3. She sleeps in a cold attic,
    Gets up at dawn each day
    And we know she never
    Has the time to play, but –

73

Ostinato accompaniment – chorus only

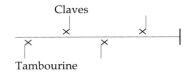

NARRATOR   One day a messenger called at the house. He brought an invitation to a Grand Ball to be held at the Palace for the birthday of the King's son.

(Messenger arrives, stepmother takes invitation)

STEPMOTHER My dears, how wonderful. You've been invited to the Palace Ball.

SISTER 1   Oh, mother, we must look our best, then the Prince will want to dance with us.

SISTER 2   I shall wear the red dress.

SISTER 1   No you won't. I want that one.

SISTER 2   Well, I shall wear the pearls then.

SISTER 1   Mother, the pearls are mine, aren't they? She can't wear them.

NARRATOR   The two sisters argued and squabbled. Dresses and necklaces, gloves and shoes were scattered all over the floor.

3. We've been invited to the Palace (Stepsisters)

Margaret Rolf

1. We've been invited to the Palace at last.
   To make us ready is quite a task.
   We'll clean our teeth
   And we'll fix our hair
   Then we're off – but first
   What shall we wear?

2. We've been invited to the Palace at last.
   To make us ready we must work fast.
   We'll paint our nails
   and we'll rouge our cheeks
   Then we're off – but quick
   We've just one week.

3. We've been invited to the Palace at last.
   To make us ready we must work fast.
   We'll buy new shoes
   And we'll book the coach
   Then we're off – but wait
   You've got my brooch.

NARRATOR   On the day of the Ball, the two sisters spent hours getting ready. Cinderella had to help them. She arranged their hair, polished shoes, tied bows and, at last, they were ready.

SISTER 1   How do we look?

CINDERELLA   You look very nice indeed. I wish I could go to the Ball too.

SISTER 2   How ridiculous! Look at your clothes. They are all worn out.

SISTER 1   Fetch my gloves, Cinderella.

SISTER 2   Cinderella, put my wrap around my shoulders.

SISTER 1   We're ready, mother.

Stepmother   You look really smart, my dears.

4. *We are off, Cinderella* **(Stepsisters and Chorus)**

Margaret Rolf

1. We are off, Cinderella
   To the Ball, Cinderella
   We are off, Cinderella
   To the dance.
   When we go, Cinderella
   You must work, Cinderella
   You must stay, Cinderella
   You've no chance.

   Please, dear sisters
   May I come too?
   I would like to go with you.

2. Wash the plates, Cinderella
   Peel the potatoes, Cinderella
   Polish brass, Cinderella
   Scrub the floors.
   When we go, Cinderella
   You must work, Cinderella
   You must stay, Cinderella
   Tidy drawers.

3. Clean the spoons, Cinderella
   Sharpen knives, Cinderella
   Black the stove, Cinderella
   Make the beds.
   When we go, Cinderella
   You must work, Cinderella
   You must stay, Cinderella
   Bake the bread.

Repeat verse 1 plus chorus, divided into two groups. Group 1 sing verse 1, group 2 sing the chorus. The accompanist plays the chorus.

Performance notes

Push towards an accent on the important words: 'off', 'ball', 'dance', etc. This contrasts with the legato 'please, dear sisters'. When the verse and chorus are well known, put the two parts together as suggested for the repeat of verse 1. The accompanist plays the chorus.

Ostinato accompaniment for the verse

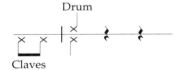

Glockenspiel accompaniment for the chorus

NARRATOR   Before the sisters left, they told Cinderella to wait up for them and not to go to sleep. They would need her help when they returned.

SISTERS 1 and 2   Goodbye, mother.

STEPMOTHER   Goodbye, my dears. Have a lovely time.
(Stepmother goes out to see the sisters off)

NARRATOR   Cinderella was so tired, she sat down near the fire. In the distance she could hear music from the orchestra at the Ball. To help cheer herself up, she did what she often did at night. She began to imagine what it was like at the Palace.

5. I sit here thinking (Cinderella and Chorus)

Gently

Margaret Rolf

CINDERELLA

1. Ev - 'ry night when I'm in bed, I think a cas - tle in my head.

I see a room all warm and light, A room where I could spend all night.

Chorus

I sit here think-ing, Think-ing, think-ing I sit here feel-ing For- got-ten and small.

I think of mu-sic and danc-ing and laugh -ter. I'd like to go to the Ball.

1. Every night when I'm in bed,
   I think a castle in my head.
   I see a room all warm and light,
   A room where I could spend all night.

I sit here, thinking,
Thinking, thinking
I sit here feeling
Forgotten and small.
I think of music and dancing and laughter.
I'd like to go to the Ball.

2. Every night when I'm in bed,
   I think a castle in my head.
   I see a room with flowers and food,
   A room with people kind and good.

3. Every night when I'm in bed,
   I think of a castle in my head.
   Beautiful ladies with princes so tall
   And gilded chairs around each wall.

Performance notes

Verse: sing this legato, moderately quietly.
Chorus: rhythmic yet lightly sung. A heavier tone is needed for 'I'd like to go to the ball'.

Percussion accompaniment

Introduction:

Chorus:

(Fairy Godmother enters during narration)

NARRATOR   As she sat sadly there, Cinderella heard a voice.

FAIRY
GODMOTHER   What is the matter, Cinderella? Why are you here when everyone else is at the Ball?

CINDERELLA   I was not invited. Who are you?

FAIRY
GODMOTHER   I am your Fairy Godmother. Just do as I say and you shall go to the Ball.

80

6. *I can make your wishes come true* (Fairy Godmother)

Margaret Rolf

FAIRY GODMOTHER

1. I can make your wishes come true.
   You can do the things you want to do.
   Don't be sad.
   Please be glad.
   I can make your wishes come true.

Performance notes

This needs to be sung with rhythmical precision. Take some time to practise the rhythm by speaking the words in time. Avoid any untidiness on the word 'true' where the 'tr' letter-blend needs to be attacked to bring everyone quickly to the 'ue' core of the word, which is held.

Please note that this song has four verses. The Fairy Godmother and Cinderella speak between each verse.

CINDERELLA   How shall I get to the Ball?
(Fairy Godmother points to a pumpkin on the floor)

FAIRY
GODMOTHER   Take that pumpkin and put it outside the door.
(Cinderella does so and returns)

2.   You must have a coach of course
From a mouse I'll make a snow-white horse.
Don't be sad.
Please be glad.
I can make your wishes come true.

FAIRY
GODMOTHER   Now go and find six mice and put them in front of the pumpkin.
(Cinderella goes outside. Fairy Godmother raises her wand.)

INTERLUDE on glockenspiel

(Cinderella returns)

FAIRY
GODMOTHER   Look outside, Cinderella.

CINDERELLA   There's a beautiful coach with six white horses. But it's no good. Look at my ragged clothes. I have nothing to wear.

82

3.	Now you need a beautiful gown.
	It will be as light as thistledown.
	Don't be sad.
	Please be glad.
	I can make your wishes come true.

FAIRY
GODMOTHER   Walk around the room, Cinderella.
(Cinderella walks around, including behind fireplace out of sight. Fairy Godmother waves wand.)

INTERLUDE on glockenspiel

(Cinderella emerges in ball gown)

CINDERELLA   Oh, Fairy Godmother, it's really beautiful. Thank you. And what lovely little shoes.

FAIRY
GODMOTHER   Now, shoo those three rats by the fireplace out into the garden.
(Cinderella does so. Fairy Godmother raises her wand.)

INTERLUDE on glockenspiel

FAIRY
GODMOTHER   Now open the door.
(Two footmen walk in and bow)

FAIRY
GODMOTHER   Now you are ready to go to the Ball. These Footmen and the coachman outside will take you there.

CINDERELLA   Thank you, Fairy Godmother.

FAIRY
GODMOTHER   Go and enjoy yourself but remember this – you must not stay at the Ball after midnight. After that everything will return to what it was before.

4.   Twelve o'clock will come all too soon.
     When it does you must be in this room.
     Don't be sad.
     Please be glad.
     I can make your wishes come true.

CINDERELLA   I'll remember. Goodbye.
(Footmen open door for Cinderella and they go out. Sounds of horses' hooves fade away.)

Scene 2 – The Palace Ballroom

(Dancers stand ready to dance)

NARRATOR   As Cinderella entered the great Ballroom, everyone turned to look at her. The Prince came over to greet her and asked her to dance.

7. Gavotte Dance for four dancers (or sets of four dancers)

Margaret Rolf

84

First Section

phrases 1 & 2   Two pairs facing each other, linking arms with partners, sufficiently far apart to take four steps towards each other.
Starting with outside foot, stepping one to a beat, move forwards: outside (foot) inside, outside, inside foot (pointing) and do this sequence backwards (starting with inside foot) into original place. Repeat.

phrases 3 & 4   Release arms and, using the same step, with outside foot leading, dance a similar sequence moving sideways away from your partner (step, close, step, close) and back again. Again repeat.

phrases 5 & 6   The dancers are now back in their original position facing the other pair. One couple carries out the first sequence again (once only) while other couple is stationary, then the other couple repeats the sequence.

Middle Skipping Section

phrases 1 & 2   On the chord, the dancers stop and turn to their partner. Link right arms and take eight skipping beats around in a clockwise motion. Turn, link left arms, and do the same the other way.

phrases 3 & 4   All four dancers join hands in a circle and skip to the left (clockwise) for eight skipping beats and then turn to the right (anti-clockwise) and skip for eight skips back to place.

Use the sustained chord, to return to original starting position and repeat the first section stopping at 'Fine'. Bow.

(Dancers move to stand in groups around the room)

Narrator   Afterwards, supper was served with lots of delicious things to eat and drink.

(Footmen with trays move amongst dancers)

Girl 1   Who is that beautiful girl who danced with the Prince?

Boy 1   I have never seen her before.

Girl 2   Someone said she is a princess.

Boy 2   She certainly makes the Prince look happy tonight.

8. Everyone's asking the question (Chorus)

Margaret Rolf

1. Ev'ryone's asking the question.
   Ev'ryone's wanting to know
   Who is the girl in the beautiful gown
   Is she a princess from out of town?
   Ev'ryone's asking the question.
   Nobody seems to know.

2. Ev'ryone's asking the question.
   Ev'ryone's wanting to know
   Why does the Prince always ask her to dance?
   Nobody else even gets the chance.
   Ev'ryone's asking the question.
   Nobody seems to know.

3. Ev'ryone's asking the question.
   Ev'ryone's wanting to know
   How we all stared as she came through the door.
   Has anyone here ever seen her before?
   Ev'ryone's asking the question.
   Nobody seems to know.

Performance notes

Take care with the ascending scale and stepwise movements to ensure that the children sing in tune. Go over the first phrase, 'Everyone's asking the question', and the phrase 'Is she a princess from out of town?' encouraging the children to smile and think the notes in the head register. Work on tuning the intervals in 'Nobody seems to know'.

NARRATOR   The Prince danced every dance with Cinderella, and she was so happy that she forgot the time. Suddenly she remembered.

CINDERELLA   What time is it?

PRINCE   It is almost midnight.

CINDERELLA   Oh no! I must go – now.

NARRATOR   Cinderella ran as fast as she could, out of the Ballroom. As she ran, she lost one of the little shoes.

(Cinderella runs out to the kitchen)

9. I must hurry (Cinderella and Chorus)

Margaret Rolf

1. I must hurry.
   I can't wait.
   I should not have stayed so late.
   I had such a lovely time
   Then I heard the clock chime.

   I must run.
   I had fun.
   I'm too late.
   I can't wait.

2. I was happy
   At the dance.
   I won't get
   Another chance.
   I was dancing –
   With the Prince
   Then I heard the clock chime.

   I must run . . .

Percussion accompaniment

Add glockenspiel to each of the four chimes, and claves to each of the phrases that follow, 'I must run' etc. And a cymbal clash on the final chord.

NARRATOR   Cinderella still had one shoe when she reached home. She hid it carefully in the kitchen and was sitting alone once more when her two step-sisters returned from the Ball.

NARRATOR   Next morning at the Palace, the Prince sent for his messenger.

PRINCE   Bring that small shoe. We shall search until we find the girl who wore it last night. I would like to make her my bride.

MESSENGER   Yes, sir. I am ready.

CRIER   O-yez, O-yez, O-yez
All the girls in the kingdom must try on the shoe. Whoever it fits will marry the Prince.

NARRATOR   For many days girls flocked to the town to try on the little shoe. Young and old, tall and short, rich and poor, thin and fat. It fitted none of them.

(Dancers form a small queue to try on the shoe which the messenger puts on a small stool, during Song 10.)

10. *Did you see a girl?* (Prince and Chorus)

Margaret Rolf

1. Did you see a girl
   Not too short or tall
   Run away from the Ball?
   She ran very quickly.
   I thought that she would fall.
   As she ran from me
   It was plain to see
   As she fled through the night
   Something strange had happened
   And she had taken fright.

   I'll go on searching.
   I'll search until I find
   The girl who I danced with.
   The girl who fills my mind.

2. She was just like a
   Fair princess and I
   Hope you know what I mean.
   We danced all the evening
   Or was it just a dream?
   As she ran away
   I could hear her say
   Oh dear! What can I do?
   Then she seemed to stumble
   And lost this little shoe.

   I'll go on searching . . .

Performance notes

Great precision is needed for the rhythm pattern 'Did you see a girl?' This contrasts strongly with the two phrases 'She ran very quickly' and 'I thought that she would fall', which need to be sung legato, as if one did not want to leave one sound before approaching the other.

NARRATOR   At last the Prince came to Cinderella's house. The sisters were so excited. The elder sister grabbed the shoe quickly and tried to stuff her large foot into it.

SISTER 1   Look. It fits me.

SISTER 2   Nonsense. Your heel is sticking out at the back. Let me try.

SISTER 1   Your toes are all bent up. It certainly does not fit you.

CINDERELLA   Please may I try it on.

SISTERS   No you can't.

PRINCE   Everyone must try. Come and see if it will fit you.

CINDERELLA   One moment, I have another one exactly like this.

(Cinderella fetches the other one and puts both shoes on. Fairy Godmother enters and waits out of sight.)

ALL   The shoe fits Cinderella.

PRINCE   I think I have found the girl I am looking for.

NARRATOR   The King and Queen welcomed Cinderella to the Palace and very soon she and the Prince were married.

Everyone in the town was invited to the celebrations but the most important guest was the Fairy Godmother.

I wonder if the two step-sisters are still arguing?

11. Cinderella's Wedding (Chorus)

Margaret Rolf

Happily
Glockenspiel

CHORUS

1. Cin - der - el - la and the Prince Will be mar - ried___ to - day. We shall all be cel - le - bra - ting

Hip, hip, hip, hoo - ray! *There'll be danc - ing in the street. Fire - works in the*

air.___ *It starts at eight. Don't be late. Ev - 'ry - one will be there.___*

CODA   *rall.*

When you hear the church bells ring - ing

Come to Cin - der - el - la's wed - ding. There'll be lots of hap - pi - ness— to share So we'll

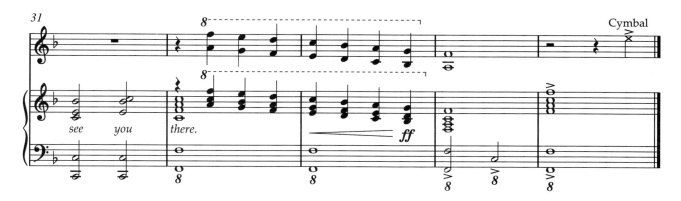

see you there. Cymbal

1. Cinderella and the Prince
   Will be married today.
   We shall all be celebrating
   Hip, hip, hip hooray!

   There'll be dancing in the street.
   Fireworks in the air.
   It starts at eight.
   Don't be late.
   Everyone will be there.

2. Bells will ring when Cinderella
   Is married today.
   Come and share the jubilation
   Hip, hip, hip hooray!

   When you hear the church bells ringing
   Come to Cinderella's wedding.
   There'll be lots of happiness to share
   So – we'll see you there.

Performance notes

As many children as possible, including instrumentalists, should be singing. An opportunity presents itself to repeat the first or second verse with the audience invited to join in.

Assessment points

What have individual children achieved with respect to their skills in:
◆ singing (expressively and competently) either as soloists or in pairs or groups?
◆ accompanying songs on untuned or tuned instruments?
◆ developing their ability to listen to and perform with other children?
◆ rehearsing towards a performance?
◆ projecting and performing to an audience?

Appendix

Transposing for vocal warm-ups

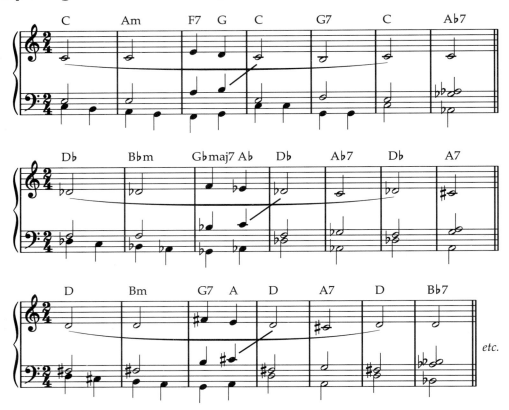

This scheme continues for each transposition; the transposition is effected by using the dominant seventh chord of the key you want to modulate to so:

Key	Transposing chord	New key
C	$A\flat^7$	$D\flat$
$D\flat$	A^7	D
D	$B\flat^7$	$E\flat$
$E\flat$	B^7	E
E	C^7	F
F	$C\sharp^7$	$F\sharp$
$F\sharp$	D^7	G
G	$E\flat^7$	$A\flat$
$A\flat$	E^7	A
A	F^7	$B\flat$
$B\flat$	$F\sharp^7$	B
B	G^7	C

The chord sequence in each key is I, VI, IV^7, V, I, V^7, I, then transpose.

Black cat (round)

I have a cat a black cat. A ve-ry fine cat in-deed.

I have a cat a black cat. A ve-ry fine cat in-

I have a cat a black cat. She's a ve-ry ve-ry ve-ry ve-ry

-deed. I have a cat a black cat. She's a

ve-ry ve-ry ve-ry ve-ry ve-ry fine cat in-deed.

ve-ry ve-ry ve-ry ve-ry ve-ry ve-ry ve-ry ve-ry ve-ry fine cat in-deed.

CD Track List

YEAR 3

13 CESARE BENDINELLI: Sonata 333 from 'A Venetian Coronation', p. 62
Gabrieli Consort and Players (Paul McCreesh)

14 GIOVANNI GABRIELI: Canzona [16] à 15 from 'A Venetian Coronation', p. 62
Gabrieli Consort and Players (Paul McCreesh)

15 MAGNUS THOMSEN: Toccata from 'A Venetian Coronation', p.62
Gabrieli Consort and Players (Paul McCreesh)

16 TRADITIONAL arr. BARRIE CARSON TURNER: 'Away in a Manger', p. 64
Barbara Law and Kate Jackson (descant recorders), William McVicker (piano), Simon Porter (percussion), Richard Jeffries (double bass)

17 JOHN STANLEY: Trumpet Tune, p. 64
London Gabrieli Brass Ensemble

18 SATIE: Gymnopédie 1, p. 64
Richard Williams (piano)

19 PAGANINI: Caprice No. 13, p. 64
Maurice Hasson (Violin)

20 GARLAND: 'In the Mood', p. 66
Glenn Miller Band

21 MERULA: 'Canzon la Ghirardella'
Amsterdam Loeki Stardust Quartet
Editions de L'oiseau-Lyre

22 HAYDN: String Quartet Op. 33 No. 4, p. 66
Lindsay String Quartet

23 STING: 'Walking on the Moon', p. 66
The Police

YEAR 4

24 VERDI: Anvil chorus from Il Trovatore
Chorus and Orchestra of the Royal Opera House, Covent Garden/Lamberto Gardelli

25 MOZART: Rondo à la Turk
Allan Schiller (piano)

26 PHILIP GLASS: Music in Twelve Parts (part 1)
The Ensemble

27 DEBUSSY: 'Footprints in the Snow'
Loris Tjeknavorian (piano)

28 MUSSORGSKY: Night on the Bare Mountain (arr. Rimsky-Korsakov)
Sydney Symphony Orchestra/José Serebrier

29 Environmental sounds, high and low pitched

30 BRAHMS: Tragic Overture
Royal Liverpool Philarmonic Orchestra/Marek Janowski

31 HOLST: 'Neptune' from The Planets
Scottish National Orchestra/Sir Alexander Gibson

32 VAUGHAN WILLIAMS: Epilogue from Sinfonia Antartica
Royal Liverpool Philharmonic Orchestra and Choir/Vernon Handley

33 LA ROCCA/EDWARDS/RAGAS/SBARBARO/SHEILDS/DE COSTA 'Tiger Rag' from At the Jazz Band Ball (Bix Beiderbecke with the Wolverines)
Recorded 20 June 1924, transfer ℗ & © 1991 Academy Sound and Vision Ltd (AJA 5080)

34 LISZT: Totentanz
Steven Mayer (piano)/London Symphony Orchestra/Tamás Vásáry

35 BACH: Orchestral Suite No. 2, last mvt.
The Brandenburg Consort/Roy Goodman

36 ANDREA AND GIOVANNI GABRIELI: 'Pater noster' from 'A Venetian Coronation' Gabrieli Consort and Players (Paul McCreesh)

37 arr. ALEX STEWART: 'The Burning Sands of Egypt'
Alex Stewart (Scottish Highland Pipes)
© Matchbox Music

38 TRAD. arr. CALICHE: 'Papel de Plata'
Caliche
© Matchbox Music

39 RĀG MALKĀUNS
Viram Jasani (Sitār), Gurdev Singh (Sarod), Ustād Latif Ahmed Khān (Tablā), Harbhajan Singh (Tānpurā)

40 Bwala Dance (Uganda)

41 Balinese Music for Gamelan Gong Gede
Gong Gede ensemble of the Temple of Batur

42 JOHN O'NEILL: 'On the Street' from The Jazz Method for Saxophone
John O'Neill (tenor saxophone)

43 JIMI HENDRIX: 'Purple Haze'
The Jimi Hendrix Experience

44 RODRIGO: 'Pequenas Sevillanas'
Carlos Bonell (Guitar)

45 POSSE: Variations on 'The Carnival of Venice'
Susan Drake (harp)

46 Drum kit
Richard Williams

47–51 Sound effects